lose wheat lose weight Cookbook

Other titles by the same author:

The Sensitive Gourmet
By Antoinette Savill

More from the Sensitive Gourmet
By Antoinette Savill

The Gluten, Wheat and Dairy-free Cookbook
By Antoinette Savill

Lose Wheat, Lose Weight
By Antoinette Savill and Dawn Hamilton Ph.D

Super Energy Detox
By Antoinette Savill and Dawn Hamilton Ph.D

lose wheat lose weight Cookbook

100 Easy Recipes for

Low Fat, Allergy-Free Cooking

Antoinette Savill

TED SMART

This edition produced for The Book People Ltd,
Hall Wood Avenue, Haydock, St Helens WA11 9UL in 2003

Thorsons
An Imprint of HarperCollins*Publishers*
77–85 Fulham Palace Road,
Hammersmith, London W6 8JB

The Thorsons website address is: www.thorsons.com

and *Thorsons*
are trademarks of HarperCollins*Publishers* Ltd

First published by Thorsons 2002

10 9 8 7 6 5 4 3 2 1

A catalogue record of this book is
available from the British Library

ISBN 0 00 767937 8

Printed and bound in China by Imago

Contents

Introduction

Lose wheat and lose weight. Could anything be that simple? The answer is, astonishingly, yes. By cutting out wheat from your daily diet, you can dramatically transform your weight and the way you feel – both physically and emotionally. Best of all, you will achieve your natural weight and sustain it, all by making some simple alterations to the way you choose to eat.

The premise behind this diet is straightforward and doesn't involve cutting down the amount you eat. In fact, with the help of some of the delicious recipes in this book, you may find you eat more and better than ever. Most diets leave you feeling hungry and depressed – weight loss may be sporadic and unlikely to last. The secret to losing weight is to change your eating habits forever; to set up new patterns of choosing and eating foods that make you feel good, keep your weight down, but, most of all, leave you feeling satisfied.

The prospect of giving up wheat may sound a daunting one. A quick read of the labels on most of your favourite foods will probably confirm that wheat is one of the mainstays of your diet, appearing in almost all of the foods that you feel you can't do without. What could be nicer than a steaming bowl of pasta, or some freshly baked bread? Could you really do without cakes, biscuits and pastries of any description? What are the options for lunch if sandwiches are out of the question? Good questions, but easily answered. You don't need to do without any of these foods – or any of your other favourites. The recipes in this book offer you not only wheat-free alternatives, but a whole host of other options that you may never before have considered. The result is a hugely exciting array of foods that will help you to create a varied diet – the very thing that will help you to overcome any food sensitivities that caused your weight problem to begin with.

Too good to be true? I assure you, it's not. Here's how it works.

The Problem with Wheat

Take a look at the meals you eat over the course of a day. Chances are, your menu looks something like this: toast and/or cereal for breakfast, biscuit midmorning, sandwich or pasta for lunch and an evening meal with pasta, bread or noodles on the side. It's possible that you have some form of wheat with virtually every meal you eat. And therein lies the problem.

Eating the same foods over and over again can lead to food intolerance. Wheat is not the only culprit – dairy foods are also common causes of intolerance as well, largely because they are so frequently overeaten. But wheat poses different problems, and we'll look at those below.

The reason why commonly-eaten foods lead to a host of debilitating symptoms is not completely understood. It is believed that overconsumption causes the digestive enzymes to malfunction. Because food is then not properly digested, health problems result. Easily-digested foods, such as fruits and most vegetables, can be dealt with by the body with ease and can therefore be eaten more frequently. However, foods that are more difficult to digest, such as wheat, are likely to cause an imbalance in enzymes and therefore an intolerance, if they are eaten too frequently.

Why Wheat?

Overconsumption is the main problem. The average western diet is based largely on wheat and wheat products. If you have ever had to shop or cook for someone with an allergy or intolerance to wheat, you will be aware of the minefield that exists. Wheat is commonly added to a wide range of processed foods and appears in almost all baked goods, and even soups, sauces and processed meats. It's easy to see how we can get too much.

Secondly, wheat is a highly-sprayed, heavily-processed crop that bears little or no resemblance to the dietary mainstay of our forebears. Spraying with pesticides, insecticides, fungicides and other agro-chemicals during the growing process contaminates the wheat and, because the kernel is so small, large quantities of these chemicals are absorbed into the grain.

Wheat germ – which contains beneficial oils, vitamin E and many of the B-complex vitamins – is stripped from the grain because it becomes rancid quickly. Most of the wheat we eat has also had the bran removed, thus reducing the fibre content of the wheat and its nourishment. Add in the other chemicals commonly used in the refining process – such as chemical oxidizing agents, bleaches, bleach neutralizers, preservatives and conditioners – and you have a toxic soup. All of these chemicals are, in small quantities, relatively unharmful, but given the amount of wheat and wheat products we ingest across the average week, month or even year, and there is no question that they will have an effect on the way our bodies function.

Every chemical with which we come into contact must be detoxified by the liver. When we take in too many chemicals, the liver is unable to cope and toxins are stored in fat cells (often over the hips and buttocks). Because resources that should be used by other parts of the body, such as the digestive system, are being diverted to the liver, everything begins to work less effectively. The result is that the body eventually becomes unduly sensitive to everyday chemicals. Equally, studies show that a single, large exposure to a toxic chemical (such as pesticides) can bring on a severe form of food intolerance. By eating a great deal of one type of food, such as wheat, we are, in reality, subjecting ourselves to massive exposure to the same chemicals.

So not only does wheat cease to be a source of useful nutrients, but it also puts a strain on the body, meaning that more and more nutrients are required for it to be digested and utilized. Although synthetic vitamins and minerals are added to most refined wheat products, these are not easily assimilated by the body, and not normally absorbed. So wheat becomes, effectively, an 'anti-nutrient' – using nutrients that should be diverted elsewhere in the body, and providing none itself.

Two parts of the wheat grain are linked to intolerance. Bran is known to irritate the digestive tract (in particular, the colon), causing symptoms such as bloating, constipation and/or diarrhoea. In many IBS sufferers, wheat is a primary cause. If bran is at the root of your problems, you may find that switching to white rather than wholemeal products will ease symptoms. However, white flour contains negligible nutrition and does not comprise a healthy form of carbohydrates.

The protein in wheat is another problem. Wheat protein (known as gluten) is made up of gliadin and glutenin. Gliadin is not easily digested, so it is one of the key problems associated with intolerance. Gliadin is present in all types of flour, so switching to white flour will not improve the problem. If you eat too much wheat, or if you are naturally short of the appropriate enzymes to digest it, protein molecules will not be broken down properly. When the colon becomes permeable (see page xii), these protein molecules can escape through the wall, into the body, triggering an immune response.

Gluten is also present in other grains (such as oats, barley and rye), but the chemical structure of the protein molecules is different in each of these. For this reason, you may find that you can tolerate these grains without any adverse side-effects.

Wheat and Weight

So how does cutting out wheat affect our weight? There are many reasons for this. First of all, when we become intolerant to a food, we tend to become bloated and retain water. This can make us appear puffy, often across the entire body, changing our shape. It also affects our weight. When many people begin the Lose Wheat, Lose Weight diet, they lose several kilograms in the first week. Much of this is water loss, but it nonetheless makes us look and feel slimmer and less bloated. The body also works more efficiently when it is not carrying excess water.

Also linked to the problem with wheat is digestive function. There are several elements to this: elimination, metabolism and the concept of leaky gut syndrome.

When we eat foods to which we are intolerant, our bodies have to work harder to cope with them. Blood sugar tends to drop (see page xxi), which leaves us with feelings of fatigue and a host of other symptoms (see page xv), all of which represent our bodies' attempts to maintain the status quo. Digestion is inefficient, so our bodies get less of the nutrients they require to work effectively.

The elimination system is also affected. Our bodies have a number of organs working to disperse unwanted chemicals and the by-products of metabolism. The liver, kidneys, lungs, digestive system, lymphatic system and skin are all involved in this process. Each system is interdependent and when one is not working effectively it places a burden on the others. Inadequate digestion causes constipation, which means that we cannot effectively eliminate wastes in this way. The liver and lymphatic system are put under additional pressure as a result and we may find that our skin becomes poor, as our bodies attempt to use this as a waste-disposal site. We may feel groggy, irritable and tired due to the increased level of toxins in the blood, and our livers are overworked in an attempt to clear the backlog. When there is no way to get rid of toxins, they are stored in fat cells. When we have a regular and high intake of chemicals (and foods to which we are intolerant, which the body treats as an invader), fat cells are created and maintained for use as a dumping ground for toxins that the body cannot deal with. Losing weight involves releasing fat cells into the bloodstream for removal via the waste disposal systems. If these are not working effectively, the body hangs on to the fat cells to prevent a toxic release that would overload and effectively poison the body.

What about metabolism? When the body has to work harder to cope with foods it finds difficult to digest – and obtains insufficient nutrients from that food – it slows down and conserves energy. The type and quality of the food we eat also has an impact on metabolism. If your diet is based around poor-quality carbohydrates, metabolism will be slower and less likely to burn up the calories of the other foods you are eating. Finally, if you experience the normal 'dip' in energy after eating wheat throughout the day, you are less likely to summon up the energy to head down to the gym or do any other form of exercise, which is essential to improving the efficiency of your metabolism.

Leaky gut syndrome is another possible problem. It is a very common health disorder in which the intestinal lining is more permeable (porous) than normal. The abnormally large spaces present between the cells of the gut wall allow toxic material – bacteria, fungi, parasites and their toxins, undigested protein, fat and waste – to leak into the bloodstream. This is material that would, in healthier circumstances, be repelled and eliminated.

Because of the spaces between the cells of the gut wall, larger than usual protein molecules are absorbed before they have a chance to be completely broken down – as occurs when the intestinal lining is intact. As a result, the immune system starts making antibodies against these larger molecules because it sees them as foreign, invading substances. The immune system then begins treating them as if they must be destroyed and makes antibodies against these proteins – proteins that are derived from previously harmless foods.

The syndrome is caused by the inflammation of the gut lining, which can be brought about by the following:

- antibiotics – because they lead to the overgrowth of abnormal flora in the gastrointestinal tract (bacteria, parasites, candida, fungi)
- caffeine and many soft drinks – these are strong gut irritants and can be particularly dangerous for younger children
- chemicals in fermented and processed food (dyes, preservatives, peroxidized fats)
- enzyme deficiencies (e.g. coeliac disease, lactase deficiency causing lactose intolerance)
- NSAIDS (non-steroidal anti-inflammatory drugs, such as ibuprofen)
- prescription corticosteroids (e.g. prednisone)
- a highly refined carbohydrate diet (including chocolate bars, sweets, cakes, biscuits, soft drinks and white bread)

The link between food intolerance and digestive function is well established, and indicates that improving digestive function and the health of the gut can have an impact on the way your body reacts to foods. In other words, by improving the health of the gut, you should be able to tolerate small amounts of the offending food without any problems. When steps are taken to address the problem, most people can overcome food intolerance fairly quickly. Your ability to lose weight is also linked with the health of your digestive system, which is why it is crucial to establish good health as a priority.

Understanding Food Intolerance

A food intolerance does not involve the immune system. It is an adverse reaction caused by specific foods. For example, lactose intolerance occurs when you lack an enzyme that is needed to digest milk sugar. Therefore, when you eat milk products, you will experience symptoms such as gas, bloating, diarrhoea and/or abdominal pain. The same holds true for wheat intolerance. For whatever reasons (poor bowel function, overeating wheat etc.), your body lacks the enzymes necessary to digest wheat, hence you will experience one of the many symptoms associated with intolerance.

Interestingly, research shows that it is almost always the most commonly eaten foods that are the source of the problem. In Britain and in other western countries, wheat and milk are key culprits, largely because they are consumed several times every day. In the US, wheat and milk are equally suspect, but sensitivity to corn is also very common, partly because it is present in so many prepared foods in the form of cornflour and corn syrup. These products are used in the UK, but to a lesser degree. Peanuts are also a very common allergen in the US – possibly because peanut butter is so popular, but also because peanuts are a very common snack food.

Dr Jonathan Brostoff and Linda Gamlin, authors of *Food Allergy and Intolerance*, reported a remarkable link between the overconsumption of particular foods and subsequent sensitivities in patients. They claim that a large intake of any food, regardless of what it is, can trigger off intolerance to that food.

Causes of Intolerance

While the immune system is not directly linked to food intolerance, there is no doubt that we can experience unpleasant symptoms when we are rundown or ill. It may be that a system under pressure is less likely to cope in the normal way with everyday foods and, as a result, symptoms develop. In such cases, it is best to withdraw any food that causes a reaction until you feel back on form.

As discussed above, some people may not have adequate amounts of some enzymes needed to digest certain foods. Insufficient quantities of the enzymes required to digest wheat, for example, make it difficult to digest the proteins in wheat (mainly gluten), resulting in symptoms.

Furthermore, food poisoning can mimic an allergic reaction. Some types of mushrooms and rhubarb, for example, can be toxic.

Bacteria in spoiled tuna and other fish can also produce a toxin that triggers adverse reactions.

There is also a peculiar psychological element to food intolerance. When you are under pressure or have had a particularly bad experience with a certain food (perhaps vomiting after eating too much), you may develop something of a phobia, with the result that the same symptoms represent themselves whenever that food is eaten. While the symptoms are undoubtedly psychosomatic, they are very real, and it can be very difficult to ascertain whether there is a genuine intolerance or it is simply a physical manifestation of an emotional problem.

Symptoms of Intolerance

Symptoms are often difficult to pinpoint, largely because they can seem innocuous in the early stages. The time it takes for symptoms to appear can also make it harder to link a reaction with a specific food. Some people become intolerant after a course of antibiotics, or following exposure to pesticides or other toxins. Symptoms may become worse in periods of stress, or after illness, which also clouds the issue.

Some of the most common symptoms include:

- anxiety
- asthma
- bloating
- chronic sniffling
- constipation
- coughing
- Crohn's disease
- diarrhoea
- eczema
- excess mucus
- facial puffiness
- fatigue
- flatulence
- headaches
- hives
- IBS
- indigestion
- insomnia
- itchy eyes
- itchy skin
- mood swings
- mouth ulcers

- muscular aches
- nausea
- skin rashes (around the mouth in particular, although the whole body may be affected)
- sore throats
- water retention
- wheezing

Do You Suffer from a Wheat Intolerance?

There are many ways to test for wheat allergies, and intolerance, but the reliability of these tests is questionable and they are often very expensive. It is just as easy to self-monitor, by keeping a food diary, and by watching carefully to see how you feel in the 48-hour period after eating foods that contain wheat of any description.

Watch out for any of the symptoms noted above, but also consider the following:

1 Do you suffer from bloating around your abdominal area for no apparent reason?
2 Do you suffer from flatulence regularly?
3 Are your bowel movements erratic (diarrhoea and/or constipation on a regular basis)?
4 Do you feel tired when you waken in the morning, even after a good night's sleep?
5 Do you have periods where you find it difficult to concentrate?
6 Do you suffer from recurrent headaches or migraine?
7 Do you have rashes, eczema, acne or more spots than usual?
8 Do you suffer from rashes and spots around your mouth and chin area?
9 Do you experience a dip in energy levels and concentration after eating foods that contain wheat?

10 Do you crave foods that contain wheat?
11 Does your weight fluctuate for no reason?

If you answer yes to more than four of these questions, and, in particular, questions 9 and 10, chances are you do suffer from some sensitivity to wheat. The best way to test for intolerance is to look for any changes in your health (particularly the symptoms described above), even if it has been a slow progressive change.

Cravings are one of the key symptoms of intolerance. Some studies show that at least 50 per cent of us suffer food cravings for problem foods. We may even be unaware of it. Take a look at your own diet and see what foods you eat most commonly. Try cutting out these foods for several weeks and see if you experience better health to any significant degree. Many people who suffer from regular headaches, low-grade niggling health problems and fatigue are intolerant or sensitive to certain foods, and it isn't until these foods are removed that they are even aware that a problem existed.

COELIAC DISEASE

The protein in wheat – gluten – is also found in other cereal grains, such as rye, oats and barley. Those who suffer from coeliac disease or 'coeliac sprue' suffer from a permanent, adverse reaction to gluten, and will not lose their sensitivity to this substance. The only treatment is lifelong avoidance of gluten – and that means any of the grains that contain it.

In contrast, those who have a wheat allergy need only avoid wheat. Confusing, it is, but there are differences between the gluten found in the various grains, and studies show that wheat-allergic people can normally eat other gluten-containing grains without any problem. Most wheat-allergic children outgrow the allergy.

The exact cause of coeliac disease is unknown. Coeliac disease develops in children (and adults) who are genetically predisposed to the condition, and occurs when eating grains containing gluten. Some children do not develop the disease until a trigger, such as a viral illness or in some cases immunization, begins the abnormal immune response.

Coeliac disease causes the intestine to lose its ability to absorb nutrients. Weight loss, anaemia and vitamin deficiencies may occur as a result of inadequate absorption of nutrients from the intestinal tract. After exposure to gluten, intestinal damage may develop within a few months or may not become evident for several years.

Because the exact cause is unknown, there is no way known to prevent the development of coeliac disease. However, awareness of risk factors (such as a family member with the disorder) may increase the chance of early diagnosis and treatment.

Total withdrawal of gluten from the diet permits the intestinal mucosa to heal and results in a disappearance of the symptoms of coeliac disease. Even within a matter of days following withdrawal of dietary gluten some symptoms improve – for instance, irritability goes away and appetite improves.

Keeping a Food Diary

In order to work out whether or not you have a food or additive intolerance, it is helpful to keep a food diary of everything that passes your lips – not just meals, but also drinks, food supplements and even water. Record the time that each is eaten or drunk, the approximate quantities, and relevant details, such as the brand and whether or not the food or drink is organic. Write all of these details on the left-hand page of a large notebook. On the right-hand page record any symptoms that you notice, the time they occur and how long they last.

At the end of a week or so, go through the diary, looking for recurring patterns. You may notice that you become slightly moody after eating toast or bread, or that you feel tired or headachy after a bowl of pasta. A sandwich might give you stomach pains, or make you feel bloated. Make a comprehensive list of every food that seems to trigger a regular pattern of symptoms. Watch out too for foods that you regularly crave, as these are likely to be the main culprits.

Cutting Out Wheat

You may find that you respond better to organic wheat products, so it is worth experimenting with this. If you do not experience the problems associated with conventionally-produced wheat products, it is acceptable to eat small quantities of organic brands.

However, there is no question that wheat is overeaten and a healthy diet involves ensuring that you get a good balance of plenty of different foods. Even those not suffering from a sensitivity to wheat would benefit from cutting down and following a more varied diet. Weight loss will undoubtedly occur when wheat is limited in the average diet – it is difficult to digest and puts strain on the body, which affects metabolism.

Remember that wheat is found in a variety of different products, and gluten is found in still more, including the following grains:

- Wheat (durum, semolina)
- Rye
- Barley
- Spelt
- Triticale
- Kamut
- Farina

The following ingredients are questionable and may contain some gluten, if they are prepared from one of the above grains:

- Brown rice syrup (frequently made with barley)
- Caramel colour
- Dextrin (usually corn, but may be derived from wheat)
- Flour or cereal products
- Hydrolysed vegetable protein (HVP), vegetable protein, hydrolyzed plant protein (HPP), or textured vegetable protein (TVP)
- Malt or malt flavouring (usually made from barley)
- Modified food starch or modified starch
- Mono- and di-glycerides (in dry products only)
- Natural and artificial flavours
- Soy sauce or soy sauce solids (many soy sauces contain wheat)
- Vegetable gum (may be made from oats)

Additional components frequently overlooked that often contain gluten:

- Breading
- Coating mixes
- Communion wafers
- Croutons
- Imitation bacon
- Imitation seafood
- Marinades
- Pastas
- Processed meats
- Sauces
- Self-basting poultry
- Soup bases
- Stock
- Stuffing
- Thickeners

The Acid-alkaline Connection

One of the key ways to encourage weight loss and avoid the side-effects commonly associated with dieting, such as headaches, bad breath, lack of energy and dull skin, is to keep the body in an alkaline state. The body's acid-alkaline balance adjusts throughout the day, depending on the types of foods we eat. Wheat and other grains, as well as proteins, leave an acidic residue when they are metabolized. Fruits and vegetables, after digestion, leave an alkaline residue. By balancing protein and grain intake with plenty of fruits and vegetables, the body is more likely to remain alkaline.

Balancing Blood Sugar

After a meal, glucose produced by the breakdown of food (digestion) is absorbed through the wall of the intestine into the bloodstream. At this point, there is, quite naturally, a high level of glucose in the blood. Your body takes what it immediately needs for energy and then produces insulin from the pancreas in an attempt to reduce the excess. Glucose that is not used for energy is changed into glycogen and stored in the liver and muscles to be used later. It is this finely-tuned system that usually keeps the glucose level in your blood at a healthy, well-balanced norm.

When the glucose level falls too low, adrenaline is released by the adrenal glands and glucagon is produced by the pancreas. Glucagon works in the opposite way to insulin and increases blood glucose by encouraging the liver to turn some of its glycogen stores into glucose to give us quick energy. Adrenaline – a hormone normally released when we are under stress – enters the bloodstream because of a blood sugar imbalance.

Blood sugar imbalance is one of the root causes of weight problems. We tend to crave foods that will give us a quick burst of energy, such as sweets, refined carbohydrates and chocolate, but these foods are not only unhealthy and often fattening, but they exacerbate the problem by sending blood sugar soaring in the short-term, followed by a crash shortly thereafter. Stable blood sugar helps us to avoid cravings, lose extra pounds with ease, and it provides a high level of energy.

To maintain a steady blood sugar level during the day you should aim to eat complex carbohydrates as part of your main meals. Together with a little protein, and eaten little and often, complex carbohydrates can make an enormous difference to the way you feel throughout the day. In fact, sometimes just an oatcake can be enough between meals to keep eating urges at bay.

In order to keep your blood sugar stable it is important to ensure that your carbohydrates are unrefined. In general terms, this means choosing 'whole' and 'brown', instead of 'white'. When you cut out wheat from your diet, you will need to choose some healthy alternatives, and the recipes in this book provide a wealth of inspiring and delicious choices. Try to choose foods that are as close to their natural state as possible – these are 'slow-releasing' carbohydrates, which means that they provide a slow but steady release of energy that helps to balance blood sugar. Beans, lentils and chickpeas are an excellent choice, as are potatoes, almost all vegetables and most fruits.

And not only do carbohydrates keep your blood sugar in balance, but they help to increase blood serotonin levels, the 'calming' brain chemical that helps to lift mood and curb appetite.

Glucose is the fastest-releasing carbohydrate because it needs no processing before it passes into the bloodstream and raises insulin very quickly. An index has been devised to measure the glucose levels of foods. Pure glucose is given a score of 100, and all foods are measured against this. This method is called the glycaemic index.

BLOOD SUGAR CHECK LIST

Answer the following questions:

1 Are you rarely wide awake within 20 minutes of rising? **yes/no**
2 Do you need tea, coffee or a cigarette to get you going in the morning? **yes/no**
3 Do you really like sweet foods? **yes/no**
4 Do you crave bread, cereal, popcorn or pasta? **yes/no**
5 Do you feel you 'need' an alcoholic drink on most days? **yes/no**
6 Are you overweight and unable to shift the extra kilos? **yes/no**
7 Do you often have energy slumps during the day or after meals? **yes/no**
8 Do you often have moods swings or difficulty concentrating? **yes/no**
9 Do you get dizzy or irritable if you go six hours without food? **yes/no**
10 Do you often find you overreact to stress? **yes/no**
11 Do you often get irritable, angry or aggressive unexpectedly? **yes/no**
12 Is your energy level less now than it used to be? **yes/no**
13 Do you ever lie about how much sweet food you have eaten? **yes/no**
14 Do you always keep a supply of sweet food close to hand? **yes/no**
15 Do you feel you could never give up bread? **yes/no**

If you answered 'yes' to eight or more of the above questions, then it is very likely that your blood sugar is fluctuating quite markedly during the day.

Glycaemic Index (GI)

This is a measurement of how quickly or slowly a food releases glucose into the bloodstream. The less refined a carbohydrate (for example, brown rice, whole grains, and vegetables) the lower the GI. The fibre contained naturally in these foods slows down the release of sugars and gives them a lower GI. Similarly, whole fruit will have a lower GI than fruit juice, because fibre slows down the absorption of sugar.

GLYCAEMIC INDEX FOR COMMON FOODS

Fast releasing		
sucrose (white sugar)	doughnuts *	croissants *
lucozade	mashed or baked potato	fizzy drinks
Cornflakes	rice cakes	cream of wheat *
French fries	Rice Crispies	biscuits (cookies) *
wheat bread *	rice, white	puffed crispbread *
bagels *	dates	macaroni & cheese *
jams & marmalade	honey	pizza, cheese *
		confectionery *
Moderate releasing		
porridge	bananas	potato, boiled
oat bran	raisins & sultanas	ice cream, low fat
wheat-free muesli	melon	oranges & orange juice
sweet potato	wheat bran *	sweet corn
rice, brown	baked beans, canned	carrots
Slow releasing		
soya beans	kidney beans	aples & apple juice
cherries	butter beans	rice bran
fructose (fruit sugar)	yogurt, low-fat	pearl barley
soya milk	chickpeas	dried apricots
lentils	rye flakes & rye bread	split peas

* Contains wheat.

The most important piece of information that has emerged from GI is that it is actually beneficial to combine proteins and carbohydrates. The presence of protein in food (either animal or vegetable) actually lowers its glycaemic index. So pulses, such as lentils, which naturally contain both protein and carbohydrate, have a low GI.

There are a number of books available that give the GI of virtually all foods, but it's worth noting here which common foods are fast-releasing, and which are slow.

CUT THE SUGAR

Diets high in sugar are also often high in fat and low in fibre. If you fill up on sugary foods, you are likely to be at risk of vitamin and mineral deficiencies that can underpin food sensitivities in the first place.

Every time you eat, your body has a choice: it can burn that food as energy or it can store it as fat. If more insulin is released, more of your food will be converted into fat. What's more, if food is actively being converted into fat, any previously stored fat fails to be broken down. So the more sugar you eat, the more insulin your body releases, and the more fat it stores.

Lowering the Fat

In any weight-loss diet, it makes sense to watch your intake of unhealthy fats. However, fat is one of the three essential macronutrients and as such is crucial to health. Eliminating fat from the diet completely is therefore not an option. Obviously too much fat is unhealthy, but given the recent emphasis on low- and no-fat foods, you'd think we'd be seeing a rapid decline in heart disease and obesity. As you've probably gathered, the population has, in fact, become fatter. Clearly eating the right foods, rather than eating no fats, ultimately makes all the difference to health.

Some fats are not only important, but are essential for health. These fats cannot be made in the body and it is therefore essential that we obtain them from our diet. Not surprisingly, they are known as 'essential' fatty acids, or EFAs.

ESSENTIAL FATS

Do you suffer from any of these symptoms?

- dry skin
- cracked skin on heels or fingertips
- hair falling out
- lifeless hair
- poor wound healing
- dandruff
- depression
- irritability
- soft or brittle nails
- allergies
- dry eyes
- lack of motivation
- aching joints
- fatigue
- difficulty losing weight
- high blood pressure
- arthritis

These are all signs of an essential fatty acid deficiency. EFAs are found in foods such as nuts, seeds and oily fish. These essential fats are a vital component of every human cell and the body needs them to balance hormones, insulate nerve cells, keep the skin and arteries supple and to keep the body warm. They also have an enormous impact on metabolism, which is, of course, crucial to weight loss.

There are three main types of fats: saturated, polyunsaturated and monounsaturated. Rather than attempting to eliminate fat from your diet, I suggest that you cut down on the unhealthy kind (saturated) and focus on the more healthy types (polyunsaturated and monounsaturated) instead.

Saturated fats

- These are the 'bad' fats, found in butter, lard, meat, hard cheeses and eggs – they are the scourge of our modern diet.
- Too much saturated fat is linked with all sorts of diseases, including heart disease, asthma and eczema, stroke, obesity and cancer.
- Saturated fat clogs our arteries and it prevents beneficial nutrients being absorbed by our bodies.

Luckily, product labelling has made it much easier for us to assess the level of saturated fats in the foods we eat. That's not to say that we need to read the labels on every single thing we eat. Choose a few products from the supermarket shelves or your cupboard at home to get an idea of the types of products that are high in saturated fats. Fried foods, mayonnaise, pizza, burgers, many baked goods such as cakes and biscuits, and cooked meats such as salami, are all high in saturated fats. These types of foods need to be kept to a bare minimum.

Another type of bad fat are the 'trans-fats', which are produced when we hydrogenate oils – even healthy oils. Hydrogenation is the process used to turn liquid fats into hard fats. Margarine is a good example of this process. A perfectly good oil is heated to give it a firmer consistency – in other words to make it more solid. We've been convinced that margarine is better for us because it uses 'healthy fats'. However, the hydrogenation process changes the nature of the fat so that our bodies cannot make use of it. Worse, it blocks the body's ability to use healthy oils. Trans-fats are used in all kinds of processed and baked food, including biscuits, pies, crisps and cakes. If you see the word 'hydrogenated' on the label, the product contains a trans-fat.

Healthy fats

All of us should aim to get more of the good fats and less of the bad fats, while cutting back on our overall fat intake. The 'good', or unsaturated, fats are broken down into two groups: polyunsaturates and monounsaturates.

The polyunsaturates include various vegetable oils, nuts, seeds and oily fish. In general the polys do not seem to cause damage in our bodies – unless they are heated, at which point they become unstable and a little more problematic. Within the polyunsaturate grouping are some fats that very good for us – the essential fatty acids (EFAs) Omega-6 and Omega-3.

- Omega-6 oils are found in nuts and seeds and also include evening primrose, starflower and borage oil. They help prevent blood clots and keep the blood thin. They can also reduce inflammation and pain in the joints and so are vital in preventing arthritis.
- Omega-3 oils are found in fish oils and linseed (flaxseed) oil and also to some extent in pumpkin seeds, walnuts and dark green vegetables. These oils can help lower blood pressure, reduce the risk of heart disease, soften the skin, increase immune function, increase metabolic rate, improve energy, help with rheumatoid arthritis and alleviate eczema. Oily fish includes mackerel, tuna, sardines, herrings and salmon.

The monounsaturated fats include olive oil, avocados, some nuts and seeds, and rapeseed oil. The monos are more stable than polys and can be heated without being adversely affected (this is the reason why so many people cook with olive oil).

Monounsaturated fats (also known Omega-9 fats) are not classed as essential fatty acids, but they can have health benefits. They have been found to lower LDL ('bad' cholesterol) and raise HDL ('good' cholesterol). Olive oil is a good example and is one of the factors that contribute to the low rate of heart disease in the Mediterranean.

When it comes to fat intake, most people are deficient in EFAs (both Omega-6 and Omega-3), and take in about three times the saturated fat they should. The balance should be as follows:

- No more than one-third of our total fat intake should be saturated (hard) fat
- At least one-third should be polyunsaturated fat, providing EFAs
- The remainder should be monounsaturated

By choosing healthy fats, and lowering your overall unhealthy fat intake, you will begin to see changes in your health, and in your weight.

Bowel health

Digestion is a crucial part of weight loss, and it is implicated in all cases of food sensitivities and intolerance. If you take steps to improve digestion, many of your symptoms – and possibly even your sensitivities – will disappear.

Friendly bacteria (known as flora) exist in the gut to help with digestion, help the body assimilate certain B vitamins, and keep unhealthy bacteria and other 'invaders' at bay. Friendly bacteria thrives when the diet includes plenty of fruit, vegetables and slow-releasing complex carbohydrates. Meat, alcohol, sugary foods and acidic grains such as wheat, deplete the friendly bacteria, as does stress, environmental pollutants and antibiotics. When healthy bacteria is depleted, you are more likely to experience digestive disorders, such as leaky gut, constipation, diarrhoea, abdominal bloating and flatulence. It is very important, therefore, to ensure that you have the correct balance of friendly bacteria.

Begin by eating live (bio) yogurt regularly. Try soya yogurts, or those made from sheep's milk or goat's milk for variety. You can also take supplemental flora, known as probiotics. Acidophilus is a good choice, and it can be taken in a variety of different forms, including as a powder, which can be sprinkled over food.

Other foods that encourage the health of the gut include blueberries, black cherries, cranberries and black grapes, all of which contain a substance that can strengthen the gut wall. Flaxseeds have a soothing and healing effect on the colon, and garlic improves the bacterial balance of the digestive tract.

Fruits, vegetables and complex carbohydrates contain high levels of soluble fibre, which can enhance the functioning of the digestive system. Ensure, too, that you get plenty of fresh water, which encourages healthy digestion.

Becoming Wheat-free

The aim is to achieve permanent weight loss, while also encouraging optimum health on all levels. You can expect to lose between one and three pounds a week (about 450g-1.4kg), although some people experience a dramatic weight loss in the first week, followed by a more gentle decline.

When wheat is removed from your diet, you may feel slightly unwell for the first few days. You might feel tired or sleepy, find it difficult to concentrate, suffer from headaches and/or feel a bit 'out of it'. This is a normal reaction – it will settle down in a few days. If you experience these symptoms, it is a fairly good sign that wheat was at the root of the problem, and that removing it will help your overall health in the long term.

After two weeks or so of living without wheat, you will become sensitized, and will find that even small quantities produce exaggerated symptoms – normally digestive complaints and a general sense of malaise. It is extremely important, therefore, to avoid all wheat at this point. If you do inadvertently eat some wheat, drink plenty of water and take it easy.

Five weeks of a wheat-free diet should make a dramatic

difference. You should feel more energetic, think more clearly, suffer from less bloating and fluid retention, and experience relief from the symptoms described on pages xv–xvi. You will also have lost weight, which will encourage a positive new approach to your body. When you start to feel well again, you can do one of two things. You can simply continue on the wheat-free diet for the medium term, or you can test out wheat again in your diet – with some toast, a sandwich, or perhaps a bowl of pasta. See how you feel for the next 48 hours. If the symptoms recur, drop the wheat again. If you feel alright, you can introduce small quantities of wheat into your diet. But try very hard not to go overboard, or you are likely to end up back at square one. The key to a healthy diet is variety, so you should eat a wide range of nutritious foods to ensure that you are getting all the nutrients you need to look and feel great.

A Healthy Diet

Choose organic foods wherever possible. Although it is undoubtedly more expensive, there is no question that it is better for your health, as it puts far less strain on your body. If all of your body systems are working efficiently, you will be much more likely to lose weight – and keep it off in the long term.

Make your diet as varied as possible. Not only will you reduce the possibility of overeating any one food, which can lead to sensitivities, but you will ensure a good range of nutrients required to keep your body working at optimum level.

Focus on vegetables and fruits as the mainstay of your diet, and add small quantities of good-quality protein, complex carbohydrates and healthy fats. Avoid refined carbohydrates, which are present in most wheat-containing foods, and anything that is processed and/or high in sugar. These affect blood sugar, which will cause cravings and make it impossible to shift pounds. Good choices of complex carbohydrates include grains, legumes, fruit, vegetables and breakfast grains such as millet flakes, buckwheat, oats, oat bran and barley flakes. Brown rice, rice noodles, lentils and potatoes with skins are also good.

As part of your weight loss plan you may want to avoid mixing certain protein foods with carbohydrates. This strategy can speed up weight loss, and is beneficial for the digestive system. As a rule of thumb, try to avoid eating meat or fish with carbohydrates such as rice and potatoes. Fruits and vegetables are acceptable with any type of meat or fish. Yogurt, cottage cheese and eggs are good sources of protein, as are nuts and seeds.

Avoid foods that are high in fat, contain refined sugar, or are high in preservatives, additives and other chemicals. Low-calorie and 'low-fat' foods are likely to contain plenty of chemicals to make them palatable. Stick to foods that are close to their natural state, or 'whole'.

REFERENCE LIST FOR DAILY & SPECIAL TREATS FOOD

When you start following the programme, it can be difficult to remember which foods can be enjoyed every day, and which should be restricted. A quick glance at this list will remind you.

	Daily	*Special treats only*
Dairy		
Cheese, low-fat cottage	✓	
Cheese, half-fat hard		✓
Crème fraîche, half-fat		✓
Eggs	✓	
Fromage frais, virtually fat-free	✓	
Ice-cream, low-fat		✓
Milk; virtually fat-free or soya	✓	
Yogurt; natural, fat-free bio, soya (natural) or Yofu	✓	

	Daily	Special treats only
Fish and Seafood All types, especially;		
Cod	✓	
Haddock	✓	
Mackerel	✓	
Salmon	✓	
Sardines	✓	
Tuna	✓	
Seafood, all types	✓	
Poultry and Game		
All lean cuts with skin removed (except roast duck and goose)	✓	
Roast duck and goose, with fat and skin removed		✓
Meat		
All very lean cuts with skin removed	✓	
Bacon, rindless grilled (broiled) back		✓
Offal, all types with fat removed	✓	
Fruit		
All fruits except, fresh dates, fresh figs, grapes, mangoes and oranges	✓	
Fresh dates, fresh figs, grapes, mangoes and oranges		✓
Vegetables		
All vegetables, including potatoes (in their skins) and sweet potatoes	✓	
Flour (wheat-free only)		
Barley *	✓	
Buckwheat	✓	
Cornflour	✓	

	Daily	*Special treats only*
Gram	✓	
Maize meal	✓	
Oat *	✓	
Polenta	✓	
Rye *	✓	
Wellfoods or other wheat-free flour	✓	
Grains		
Barley *	✓	
Buckwheat	✓	
Millet flakes	✓	
Oats *	✓	
Quinoa and Quinoa flakes	✓	
Brown or wild rice, also rice flakes	✓	
Rye flakes *	✓	
Pulses		
All pulses, especially:		
Broad beans	✓	
Chickpeas	✓	
Kidney beans	✓	
Lentils	✓	
Nuts (moderate quantity)		
Almonds, unblanched	✓	
Brazil nuts	✓	
Hazelnuts, in their skin	✓	
Macadamia nuts		✓
Pecan nuts	✓	
Pine nuts	✓	
Pistachios		✓
Walnuts	✓	

	Daily	*Special treats only*
Bottles and Jars		
Cold pressed extra virgin olive oil, sunflower oil (moderate quantity)	✓	
Natural and wheat-free sauces	✓	
Seeds (moderate quantity)		
All seeds, especially:	✓	
Flax (linseed)	✓	
Pumpkin	✓	
Sesame	✓	
Sunflower	✓	
Sprouted Seeds		
All sprouting seeds, especially:		
Alfalfa	✓	
Mung	✓	
Vegetarian (wheat-free products only)		
Soya products*	✓	
Tofu (bean curd)	✓	
Miscellaneous		
Flavourings (natural and wheat-free) *	✓	
Herbs, all	✓	
Pasta (wheat/gluten-free) dried or fresh	✓	
Rice noodles, dried or fresh	✓	
Spices*	✓	

*The following flour contains gluten: barley, oat and rye. The following grains contain gluten: barley, oats and rye flakes and must be avoided by coeliacs. Flavourings, sauces, spices and vegetarian products also contain gluten and must be replaced with gluten-free products.

FOODS TO AVOID

	Avoid completely	*Moderate use only*
Dairy		
Butter	✓	
Cream/cream products	✓	
Full-fat cheeses/cheese products	✓	
Full-fat sweetened yogurts & desserts	✓	
Full-fat ice cream & frozen desserts	✓	
Eggs		
Mayonnaise	✓	
Custard	✓	
Fried eggs and scrambled eggs	✓	
Nuts		
Cashew nuts	✓	
Peanuts	✓	
Coconut	✓	
Coconut milk (30% reduced fat)		✓
Fats		
Lard	✓	
Margarine	✓	
Nut butters (e.g. peanut butter)	✓	
All processed meats and sausages	✓	
Items containing sugar		
Alcohol		✓
Chocolate & sweets	✓	
Dried fruits		✓
Honey		✓
Jams and spreads	✓	
Maple syrup		✓

	Avoid completely	Moderate use only
All sugar	✓	
Ready-made cakes, biscuits cookies, pastries, muffins, doughnuts, puddings and sauces	✓	
Miscellaneous		
Salt	✓	
Crisps and chips	✓	
Orange juice	✓	
Fizzy drinks and sweetened drinks	✓	

As these foods and liquids should be completely avoided none of the above list has been indicated as containing gluten or wheat.

60 FOODS THAT CONTAIN WHEAT

This list refers to standard supermarket products. Bread, for instance, means the standard loaf, not rye bread or other specialized breaths. Where the item specifies 'most' or 'many' please read the ingredients label to check whether wheat has been used. It is very important to check the labels of all processed foods, as wheat is frequently added. It may be listed as starch or modified starch.

Bagels
Batter
Biscuits/Cookies (all)
Bread (all)
Bread sticks
Breakfast cereals (many)
Bulgar wheat
Cakes and Muffins (all)
Chapatti
Crispbread (most)
Croissants
Crumble mix
Cake and muffin mix
Cauliflower cheese
Chocolate bars and sweets (candy)
Cheese biscuits (crackers) and
Twiglets
Couscous
Curry sauce and chilled/frozen curries
Custard powder or sauce

Doughnuts
Dumplings
Durum wheat
Danish pastries
Egg noodles
Fish cakes or fish fingers
Fish in batter or breadcrumbs
Fish pie
Frozen desserts
French bread and French toast
Gravy powder
Macaroni cheese and Lasagne
Mayonnaise (some)
Meat pies and puddings
Mexican dishes such as enchiladas, wheat flour tortillas and nachos
Naan bread
Onion bhajis (but wheat-free in most Indian restaurants)
Pancakes or crêpes
Pasta (all)
Pasta sauce (many)
Pastry
Pitta bread
Pizza crusts or bases
Pot noodles
Quiches
Sausages and sausage rolls
Seafood in breadcrumbs
Scotch eggs
Semolina
Soup (most)
Spring rolls
Sauce mix (most)
Steamed puddings
Scones and crumpets
Sliced processed ham, turkey and meats
Vegetables in batter (e.g. onion rings)
Vegetables in breadcrumbs (e.g. mushrooms)
Vegetarian frozen dishes (most)
Vegetarian prepared foods (most)
Waffles
Yorkshire puddings

Eat regularly, and when you are hungry. Always drink plenty of fresh water. Some of the time, what we consider to be hunger is, in fact, thirst. If you are well hydrated, you will only feel hungry when you actually need food. Furthermore, water is essential for healthy digestion, and it will help your body to eliminate toxins that are released from your fat stores as you begin to lose weight.

Learn to listen to your body. If you feel a dip in energy, choose a good-quality, complex carbohydrate snack. Seeds and nuts, such as almonds, are a good choice, or a piece of fruit or some crudites. Don't ever let yourself get so hungry that you reach that 'shaking', 'starving' state, where you'll eat whatever is to hand. No successful diet should ever leave you feeling hungry.

Always eat breakfast, whether you are hungry or not. Your blood sugar will be very low after a night without food, and your body needs fuel to operate properly. This will also prevent you from snacking on inappropriate foods later in the day.

Make your diet a priority. Plan meals in advance, consider what you are eating on a daily and weekly basis. No day will ever be perfect, but you can balance a few bad days or weeks by choosing fresh, wholesome foods the rest of the time. And if you know in advance what you are likely to be eating, and have the ingredients to hand, you'll be less tempted by unhealthy treats.

Consider the benefits of a healthy detox programme to energize and invigorate. My book *Super Energy Detox* provides details of an exciting new detox, and can be used before or, from time to time, within the wheat-free diet. Try to take on board some of the elements of detoxing in your daily life – brush your skin to help move the lymph, clear cellulite and improve elimination. Have a day, or a couple of days, where you eat only fruits and vegetables (and their juices), for a great nutritional boost, and a gentle 'clearing' of the system.

Be as active as possible. Exercise encourages every part of your elimination system, and it speeds up your metabolism. It also leaves you feeling invigorated, and helps to set up healthy sleep patterns.

Most importantly, however, enjoy! Take pleasure in what you eat.

Actively seek out delicious treats and sit down to savour them. Healthy eating does not have to be boring – in fact, it is quite the opposite. Most processed and ready-prepared foods are bland or overseasoned, to make up for poor quality ingredients. In time, you'll get used to – and love – the natural sweetness and flavour of fresh, whole foods. You'll find that your cravings disappear, and your palate changes completely – you'll no longer want or need wheat on a daily basis.

Finally, embrace your new lifestyle with a positive attitude. Cutting out wheat may seem to be an impossible hurdle, but it becomes easier and easier with time. As you continue, you will feel a host of wonderful benefits that will encourage you on your journey towards optimum health and finding your natural weight. The recipes in this book will provide inspiration when you feel stuck, and they offer delicious, nutritious and tempting alternatives to traditional dieting fare. You will find you are eating better than ever before, and experimenting with different types of foods and tastes.

Try foods that you may not have tasted before, and savour the original combination of ingredients. Not only will you lose weight, as you lose wheat, but you'll feel better than you ever have before – and acquire a gourmet's palate in the process.

Introduction to the Recipes

The delicious wheat-free recipes featured in this book are designed to make following a wheat-free and healthy diet pure pleasure. They will not only encourage weight loss, they will help you enjoy maintaining your healthy lifestyle.

You may from time to time wish to boost your weight loss – if so, follow the diet programme in *Lose Wheat, Lose Weight* (also published by Thorsons). With this book, you now have a much larger selection of recipes to choose from, so you can either dip back and forth between the two books, or just stick to these delicious recipes.

In these recipes I have aimed to use wheat-free ingredients but, as they are tailored primarily to readers who are avoiding wheat in order to lose weight, they do include some ingredients that contain tiny amounts of starch (for instance, Worcestershire sauce, soy sauce, baking powder, mixed spice and mustard). For most people, these ingredients are fine in such small amounts, but they must not be used by anyone with an allergy or severe intolerance to wheat. Items that may contain gluten are marked with an asterisk (*) in the ingredient column. You will, however, be able to find gluten-free alternatives in health food shops.

You will find the recipes arranged in groups, but do not be bound by this – they can be used in many different ways. For example, all the starters can be served as main courses for fewer people. The recipe for Lemon and Caper Stuffed Pears, for example, will serve two as a main course with a mixed salad, or four, as suggested, if used as a starter. I have also suggested alternative ingredients wherever possible to allow you to make the recipe lots of times without getting bored. The recipe for Fish Pie with Asparagus and Celeriac, for example, can be made with white fish, smoked haddock or wild salmon, as the mood takes you.

It is very useful to have a big clearout of your kitchen cupboards, refrigerator and freezer before you embark on a wheat-free lifestyle. Throw away any products that contain wheat, so you can start afresh and replace any products you need for these new recipes. If you are very busy – or very organized – you may want to make a menu for the week and write a shopping list based on this. That way your diet plan is less likely to go off track. You will also find that this helps you to balance out your meals so that you can have special treats over the week, not all in one go!

All these recipes will ensure that you will not feel deprived. Some are specifically for entertaining and special occasions – which is when it is particularly tempting to stray. If you are entertaining, don't see it as an excuse for a blowout. By all means have a three-course menu but balance the meal by having a light starter and pudding so that you can have a richer main course, or have a naughty pudding and light starter and main course – whatever takes your fancy.

The ingredients in this book are available from major supermarkets and health food stores. For those who live in the countryside, where it may prove more difficult to find some of these products, I have provided a list of companies that have mail order and Internet delivery services. Obtaining good quality wheat-free flour from supermarkets can be a particular problem. Many types of wheat-free flour were tested for these recipes. The best results came from Wellfoods flour, which produced a light texture and good colour that are less usual with other brands. This is the flour I used in all the recipes. It is gluten-free and available by mail order from Wellfoods Ltd. Any good quality wheat or gluten-free flour mix can be used, but please be aware that the absorbency of every flour is different so you may need to add a little more liquid if the mixture is too stiff, or add a little more flour if the mixture is too soft or runny. For emergencies, it is a good idea to have a supply of wheat- or gluten-free bread that you can freeze in slices or wheat- or gluten-free bread rolls that can be used for snacks or in the recipes.

I hope that these little snippets of information help you to make the most of your wheat-free diet and – most of all – that you really enjoy cooking and eating all of these recipes.

Cookery Notes

Throughout this book, solid and liquid ingredients are given in metric and US measures. Please use one set of measures only, as they are not interchangeable. All recipes have been tested twice, using metric measures and US measures.

- Unless otherwise stated, eggs are assumed to be medium sized.
- Cups and spoons are assumed level unless otherwise stated.
- Where no weight is given for meat, portions are assumed to be standard sized.
- All the recipes can be made by anyone with a reasonably well-equipped kitchen. Where any unusual equipment or a dish of a specific size is needed it is listed in the ingredients column.

A Note for Coeliacs

If you are a coeliac, you can use the recipes in the book. I have indicated any ingredient that does, or may, contain gluten with an asterisk (*), so that a gluten-free substitute can be purchased and used in the recipe. You should not use any ingredient that may contain gluten, so please check every label carefully. The ingredients and foods that I have used throughout the book are wheat-free, or with such small amounts of starch that they can be part of the wheat-free diet plan, but not part of a gluten-free diet.

At-a-glance DO'S and DON'TS list

DO	DON'T
Enjoy a pudding from time to time	Snack on breads, biscuits, doughnuts, pastries and chocolate
Avoid mixing meat, chicken, fish or seafood with carbohydrates	Add more salt to your food, just season the recipes lightly
Eat fish at least three times a week	Eat meat more than twice a week
Chew your food, eat it slowly and really enjoy it	Bolt your food
Prepare food without nibbling	Eat leftover food from lunch, tea or dinner parties

ESSENTIAL SUPPLIES

These are the most useful foods to keep in your store cupboard, refrigerator or freezer. Buy organic produce whenever possible – not only is the flavour and texture so much better but all the chemical sprays, additives and preservatives are also avoided.

- Gluten-free and wheat-free* flour such as Wellfoods or Doves Farm*
- Wheat-free baking powder* and bicarbonate of soda
- Wheat-*/gluten-free sliced bread
- Antoinette Savill range of gluten-free breads, bread rolls and pizza
- Wheat-free ratafias *
- Wheat-*/gluten-free spaghetti and different styles of pasta
- Rice noodles
- Risotto, brown and wild rice
- Almonds and ground almonds
- Sesame and poppy seeds
- Ready-to-eat dried peaches, figs, sultanas, raisins and other fruits
- Clear organic honey and maple syrup
- Organic soya milk or virtually fat-free milk, live natural yogurt or Yofu, ice cream, virtually fat-free fromage frais, half-fat crème fraîche, reduced fat or vegetarian hard cheese or cottage cheese
- Free-range eggs (organic if possible)
- Frozen raspberries, strawberries and berry mixtures
- Frozen organic vegetables such as broad beans, peas and green beans
- Frozen prawns
- Frozen individually-wrapped chicken breasts and salmon fillets
- Fresh root ginger, chillies and garlic
- Fresh lemons, limes and oranges
- Good quality pesto
- Mixed dried herbs, fresh herbs and some spices*
- Worcestershire sauce* and soy sauce*
- Balsamic vinegar, cold pressed extra virgin olive oil, cold pressed sunflower oil and organic sunflower oil

Marigold vegetable bouillon powder or other cubes of stock powder* or paste*
Dried wild mushrooms
Canned anchovies, artichoke hearts, chickpeas and lentils
Marsala, extra dry white vermouth, red vermouth and red and white wine

* Coeliacs please use gluten-free ingredients

soups

Pickled Ginger, Lemon Grass and Mussel Soup

Serves 6

In this recipe the impact of pickled ginger is balanced by the subtle flavour of fresh lemon grass. I keep both in the refrigerator for stir-fries and curries.

1 tablespoon sesame oil
6 spring onions, chopped
1 red chilli, seeded and chopped
2 garlic cloves, peeled and crushed
2 lemon grass stalks, finely sliced
1kg/2¼ lb prepared fresh (or frozen) mussels in or out of shells
425g/15oz can condensed beef consommé
600ml/2½ cups water
140g/5oz pickled ginger slices in rice vinegar, drained
1 teaspoon fish sauce* (or double up on gluten-free soy sauce)
1 teaspoon dark soy sauce*
Sea salt and freshly ground black pepper
1 bunch fresh coriander, chopped

*Coeliacs please use gluten-free ingredients

Heat the oil in a large pan. Add the spring onions, chilli, garlic and lemon grass and cook for 3 minutes.

Add the mussels, followed by the consommé, water, pickled ginger, fish sauce and soy sauce. Season with a little salt and pepper and simmer for 10 minutes.

Serve the soup immediately in hot bowls, sprinkling each serving with the chopped coriander.

Courgette Soup Serves 6

This Italian recipe is simple and delicious, as well as being suitable for all the family.

Soup

1 tablespoon cold pressed extra virgin olive oil
2 garlic cloves, peeled and chopped
1kg/2¼ lb courgettes, sliced
Sea salt and freshly ground black pepper
1 litre/4 cups vegetable stock*
1 tablespoon half-fat crème fraîche (optional)
A small handful of fresh basil leaves, chopped

Crostini (optional)

6 slices of wheat* or gluten-free white bread, crusts removed (see page 175 for brands and stockists)
18 pitted black olives*
½ mild fresh chilli, seeded
2 tablespoons cold pressed extra virgin olive oil
1 heaped tablespoon freshly chopped parsley leaves

*Coeliacs please use gluten-free ingredients

Heat the oil in a large saucepan, add the garlic and courgettes and cook slowly for about 35 minutes, or until the courgettes are soft and golden, stirring from time to time to make sure that they do not stick to the pan. Add the salt, pepper and stock and simmer for another 25 minutes.

Meanwhile, make the crostini. Cut the bread into circles with a large pastry cutter or into simple triangles if you prefer. Mix the olives, chilli, olive oil and parsley together in a food processor and whiz until it reaches the consistency of a spread.

Remove the soup from the heat and cool until it is safe to liquidize to a purée. Return the soup to the pan, stir in the créme fraîche and basil and adjust the seasoning if necessary.

Toast the bread under the grill on a baking tray. When the bread is golden on one side, remove the tray of toast from the heat. Spread the olive mixture on the uncooked side of the bread, return to the grill and heat through until the edges are golden. Serve the crostini beside each bowl of soup.

Chilled Prawn and Cucumber Soup Serves 6–8

This is a simple summer soup, refreshing and light but smart enough for entertaining – a sort of prawn gazpacho without the fat and calories. Please keep this soup in the refrigerator until needed, as shellfish can be so susceptible to the effects of hot sunshine.

1¾ large cucumbers, peeled and diced
400ml/1¾ cups vegetable stock* or cold water
125ml/½ cup chilled tomato juice
1 red chilli, seeded and finely chopped
1 garlic clove, peeled and crushed
500ml/2 cups fat-free natural yogurt
225g/8oz peeled and chopped cooked prawns, chilled
Sea salt and freshly ground black pepper
2 tablespoons chopped fresh mint leaves
¼ cucumber, to garnish
6–8 whole cooked prawns, to garnish

*Coeliacs please use gluten-free ingredients

Put the diced cucumber in a food processor with the stock or water and process until it becomes a fine purée.

Transfer the mixture to a large serving bowl and stir in the tomato juice, chilli and garlic. Mix in the yogurt, chopped prawns, salt, pepper and chopped mint – and taste it! Cover the soup with clingfilm and chill for a couple of hours to allow the flavours to develop.

Decorate the chilled soup before serving. First, wipe clean the skin of the remaining cucumber quarter, and then cut it into 12–16 thin slices. Place two overlapping slices of cucumber in the centre of the soup and place one of the reserved prawns on top.

Celeriac and Watercress Soup Serves 6

Celeriac is much easier to buy now than it was, which is great because I love the gentle taste and texture. It is an excellent light, low calorie substitute for mashed potatoes or parsnips – as well as making delicious salads and soups.

1 tablespoon cold pressed extra virgin olive oil
1 celeriac (about 680g/1lb 8oz), peeled and chopped into small cubes
1 large onion, sliced
1125ml/4½ cups vegetable stock*
2 x 85g/3oz packets prepared watercress
Sea salt and freshly ground black pepper
Freshly grated nutmeg
About 250ml/1 cup virtually fat-free milk

*Coeliacs please use gluten-free ingredients

Heat the oil in a pan over medium heat, add the celeriac and onions and cook gently until softened but not browned. Stir in the stock and simmer for about 25 minutes. Add the watercress and season with a little salt, pepper and nutmeg. Let the soup cool and then liquidize until smooth with the milk.

Transfer the soup back to the pan, adjust the seasoning to taste and reheat gently. Do not boil the soup or it may separate.

Artichoke Soup Serves 8

Artichokes are full of wonderful things that help fight off colds and generally stop you feeling under the weather. So here is a hearty and warming soup that might help you feel good on a gloomy winter's day.

Soup

2 onions, thinly sliced
16 large Jerusalem artichokes, peeled and sliced
1 tablespoon vegetable stock powder*
2 litres/2 quarts water
3 bay leaves
2 heaped teaspoons dried mixed herbs
I garlic clove, peeled and crushed
I small mild chilli, seeded and chopped
I tablespoon wheat-free cornflour*
Sea salt and freshly ground black pepper
400g/14oz can artichoke hearts, drained and quartered

Green sauce

15g/½ oz fresh basil, with stalks
15g/½ oz fresh parsley, with stalks
15g/½ oz fresh coriander, with stalks
2 tablespoons balsamic vinegar
4 tablespoons water
Sea salt and freshly ground black pepper

*Coeliacs please use gluten-free ingredients

Place the onions, Jerusalem artichokes and stock powder in a large pan. Add the water, cover, bring to the boil and cook for 6 minutes. Drain away the water and return the onions and artichokes to the pan. Once again cover with the same amount of fresh water and, this time, add the bay leaves, herbs, garlic and chilli.

Return the pan to medium heat and bring the soup to the boil, then reduce the heat and simmer gently until all the vegetables are very soft. Let the soup cool and then liquidize it until smooth. Place the soup back on a medium heat.

Dissolve the cornflour in 1 tablespoon of cold water and stir the mixture into the soup. Bring the soup to the boil, stirring occasionally, then turn the heat down and simmer for a couple of minutes. Season to taste with salt and pepper.

Make the green sauce in a food processor. Trim the ends off the fresh herb stalks and purée the leaves and the remaining stalks with the vinegar, water and a little salt and pepper. Transfer the green sauce to a small bowl.

Stir the drained artichokes into the soup and let them heat through. Serve the soup piping hot with a swirl of tangy green sauce in the centre.

Crab Bisque Serves 2

We often go to the fisherman's house in the village where my parents live in Norfolk and buy freshly prepared Cromer crabs on the morning they were caught. They are unbelievably different from the ones you can buy in the supermarket – they're light, moist and with a taste of the sea.

½ onion, very finely sliced
1 celery stick, finely sliced
625ml/2½ cups ready-made fish stock*
2 teaspoons wheat-free cornflour*
60ml/¼ cup extra dry white vermouth
Juice of ¼ lemon and a little extra if necessary
1 prepared cooked crab in its shell
1 teaspoon tomato purée
Sea salt and freshly ground black pepper
Freshly grated nutmeg
2 teaspoons good brandy
A little chopped fresh parsley

*Coeliacs please use gluten-free ingredients

Place the onion, celery and fish stock in a pan and cook over medium heat until the vegetables are soft and half the stock has evaporated. Mix the cornflour and the vermouth together in a little cup and then stir the mixture into the stock. Bring to the boil, reduce the heat to low and, stirring all the time, gradually add the lemon juice. Simmer for a couple of minutes as it thickens.

Stir the crab meat (discard the shell) into the soup. Stir in the tomato purée and cook for another couple of minutes.

Remove the soup from the heat, season to taste with salt, pepper and nutmeg and leave to cool. Once it is cool, blend it in the liquidizer until smooth.

Transfer the soup back to the pan and reheat gently. Adjust the seasoning if necessary – sometimes it does need a bit more lemon juice too. Stir in the brandy and serve the soup hot, sprinkled with a little parsley.

Clam Soup Serves 6

This particularly light version of the all-American soup, made with fresh clams and canned tuna, is a complete low-fat meal in itself.

1 large onion, very finely chopped
1 litre/4 cups water
1 litre/4 cups fish stock*
2 garlic cloves, peeled and crushed
2 bay leaves
1 sprig fresh thyme
140ml/⅔ cup good white wine (Burgundy is perfect)
200g/7oz can tuna in brine or water, drained
A few drops of chilli sauce* or minced chilli in oil
1kg/2¼ lb fresh clams (shells on)
6 large sprigs of fresh parsley, finely chopped

*Coeliacs please use gluten-free ingredients

Put the onion and water into a large pan over high heat, cover with a lid and bring it to the boil. Cook for 5 minutes and then drain away the water. Put the onions back into the pan and once again cover them with the same amount of fresh water. This time add the stock as well and cook over medium heat for about 10 minutes.

Add the garlic, bay leaves, thyme and wine and simmer for another 10 minutes. Reduce the heat and simmer until the onions are soft and the liquid has reduced by about half. Mix in the tuna, chilli sauce or minced chilli, clams and half the parsley and simmer gently until the clams are heated through. Do not boil the soup or the clams will become rubbery. Serve the soup immediately with the remaining fresh parsley sprinkled over.

Chilled Tomato and Beetroot Soup

Serves 6 /

This soup makes a nice change from Borsch. You can use fresh beetroot but I have cheated here and used prepared ones. Do not use beetroot in vinegar as it affects the taste of the soup.

2 tablespoons cold pressed extra virgin olive oil
1 large onion, finely chopped
2 celery sticks, chopped
1 garlic clove, peeled and crushed
1kg/2¼ lb ripe vine tomatoes, skinned
310g/11oz cooked prepared beetroot*, skinned and chopped
A handful of fresh basil leaves
1 teaspoon ground cumin
Sea salt and freshly ground black pepper
850ml/3¾ cups vegetable stock*
A little virtually fat-free fromage frais (optional)

*Coeliacs please use gluten-free ingredients

Heat the oil in a large pan, add the onion and celery and cook until softened. Add the garlic, tomatoes, beetroot, basil, cumin, salt, pepper and stock, and bring to the boil.

Cook over medium heat for about 35 minutes. Cool and liquidize until smooth.

Return the soup to the pan to reheat and adjust the seasoning if necessary. Serve with a dollop of fromage frais.

Chilled Tomato and Avocado Soup

starters

Mushrooms in Pesto Serves 4–6

Serve the mushrooms hot or warm with warm, wheat-free garlic bread*. Mushrooms in pesto are delicious served with a large mixed salad but there is no need to dress the salad as the pesto does this nicely.

1kg/2¼ lb fresh button mushrooms
115g/4oz carton fresh deli pesto
Sea salt and freshly ground black pepper
Handful of fresh basil leaves, roughly chopped
Baby mixed salad leaves such as rocket, lambs lettuce and spinach (optional)

*Coeliacs please use gluten-free ingredients

Wipe the mushrooms clean and trim the stalks if necessary. Place the mushrooms in a pan of boiling salted water and boil for 3 minutes. Transfer the mushrooms to a salad bowl or dish, mix in the pesto and season with salt and pepper.

Serve the mushrooms hot sprinkled with the basil, or serve them warm on a bed of prepared salad leaves.

Polenta Canapés with Artichoke and Pesto

Serves 6 as a starter or makes 24 canapés

Canapés are great for drinks parties. For a colourful and tempting display, serve these on a large plate with the Red Pepper Polenta Canapés (see page 25). You can also serve this dish as a main course for lunch, accompanied by a couple of salads such as tomato and basil and a big green leaf and herb salad.

500g/1lb 2oz block ready-made 100% pure organic polenta
425g/15oz can artichoke hearts, drained and quartered
A sprinkling of dried flaked or crushed chilli
1 small carton (115g/4oz) fresh pesto
Sea salt and freshly ground black pepper
1 very small handful per person of prepared mixed baby salad leaves (such as rocket, spinach, watercress and frisée)
A little bottled fat-free French dressing

Cut the block of polenta into 12 equal slices across the block. Cut them vertically in half and you will have 24 canapé bases. Grill the polenta pieces on one side until golden and crispy with browned edges; turn them over and grill until golden.

Meanwhile, empty the pesto into a small bowl and stir in the chilli flakes and a little salt and pepper.

Place a quarter of an artichoke heart and a little blob of pesto on each polenta canape and grill until bubbling and hot.

Meanwhile, arrange the salad leaves on each plate and drizzle with a little fat-free dressing. Quickly transfer four of the hot polenta canapés on to each salad and serve straight away.

Red Pepper Polenta Canapés

Serves 6 as a starter or makes 24 canapés

Now that you can easily buy ready–made polenta in blocks in the supermarket, I find that I cook with it a lot more. An organic version is available, although you may have to go to a good health food shop for this.

1 tablespoon cold pressed extra virgin olive oil and a little extra for brushing
½ a red onion, very finely sliced
2 large sweet red peppers, halved and seeded
2 tablespoons balsamic vinegar
Sea salt and freshly ground black pepper
500g/1lb 2oz block ready-made 100% pure organic polenta

Heat the oil in a small pan, add the onions and gently cook them over medium heat until soft and golden but not dark. Meanwhile, brush the skin of the peppers with the extra oil and grill, skin side up, under high heat until blackened in big patches.

Remove the peppers and allow them to cool before carefully peeling off the skins with a sharp knife. Finely slice the peppers and stir them into the onions. Stir in the vinegar, salt and pepper, and let the mixture simmer until all the liquid is absorbed and the peppers are very soft and nearly mushy.

Cut the polenta into 12 equal slices across the block and then in half vertically so that you have 24 canapés. Brush both sides of the polenta with some of the extra oil and grill them under high heat until golden. Turn the polenta canapés over and grill until slightly browned at the edges.

Meanwhile, very finely chop the onions and peppers in a food processor but do not make a purée. Arrange the hot pieces of polenta on a serving plate and spoon the pepper mixture on top of each one. Decorate the canapés to suit the occasion and serve them warm.

Grilled Peppers with Anchovies and Capers

Serves 4

For the past 80 years, my family have had a little house perched on top of a mountain just over the Italian border. A tiny road zigzags up with hairpin bends and only a few passing points that leave you nervously peering down at the distant sparkling Mediterranean sea.

My grandmother used to make us dishes like this, which we ate on the terrace before the perilous journey down to the beach.

4 red and 4 yellow sweet peppers, halved and seeded
2 tablespoons capers* in wine vinegar
55g/2oz anchovies
1 large garlic clove, peeled and crushed and a little extra for the toasts
A large handful of fresh basil leaves
Freshly ground black pepper
A drizzle of cold pressed extra virgin olive oil and a little extra
2–4 slices of wheat-free white bread*, crusts removed (see page 175 for brands and stockists)

*Coeliacs please use gluten-free ingredients

Grill the peppers skin side up until they are softened and blistered all over with black patches. Allow them to cool then peel off the skin with a sharp knife.

Lay the peppers in a serving dish, cover with a sprinkling of capers, anchovies, garlic, basil and black pepper and drizzle with some oil.

Cut the slices of bread in half or cut circles with a medium-sized metal pastry cutter. Grill one side until pale gold. Remove the toast from the grill, brush the untoasted side of the bread with the extra oil and garlic and grill until golden.

Serve the toasts with the dish of peppers.

Smoked Salmon and Caper Roulade Serves 6

Just because you are watching your diet it doesn't mean that you can't have a party. You can't fail to impress with this roulade, as it is rather luxurious and elegant. It is not cooked like other roulades, so it is quick and easy to prepare, and can be made a day in advance.

400g/14oz sliced best-quality smoked salmon
11.7g sachet/US 1 tablespoon powdered gelatine, dissolved as instructed on the pack (or vegetarian equivalent)
Sea salt and freshly ground black pepper
2 tablespoons capers* in wine vinegar, drained
500ml/2 cups half-fat crème fraîche
Handful of prepared rocket leaves, to garnish (optional)

*Coeliacs please use gluten-free ingredients

Lay out the sliced salmon in strips on a sheet of clingfilm that is a little longer than the lengths of the salmon. Make sure there are no gaps and that you have a neat rectangle of salmon. Trim the edges of the salmon if necessary and use to fill in the ends so that they make a really neat rectangle.

In a mixing bowl, blend the slightly cooled gelatine with the salt and pepper, capers and crème fraîche and chill until it starts to set. Spread the thick mixture over the salmon and roll up tightly in the clingfilm. Twist the ends around like a cracker and fold the ends neatly underneath. Chill until needed.

Carefully unwrap the roulade and, using a very sharp knife, slice it up onto eight plates. I think two slices each look nice, or three very little ones are fun too. Decorate with a little rocket – and remember to serve it without bread and butter!

Asparagus and Mushroom Crostini Serves 4

You can make this dish as a main course simply by trebling up on the salad base and adding another 100g/3½ oz of mushrooms to the given quantity. It is delicious accompanied by a side plate of sliced vine tomatoes and freshly shredded basil leaves.

2 tablespoons cold pressed extra virgin olive oil, plus extra for drizzling
340g/12oz small cultivated mushrooms, wiped clean and stalks trimmed
A large pinch of dried thyme
Sea salt and freshly ground black pepper
Freshly grated nutmeg
2 x 100g/3½ oz packets prepared asparagus tips
4 x 2cm/¾ in thick slices of white wheat-free* or gluten-free bread, crusts removed
½ garlic clove, peeled and crushed
A drizzle of truffle oil
A very small handful of prepared mixed baby salad leaves (such as rocket, spinach, frisée)
A little bottled fat-free French dressing
1 tablespoon freshly chopped flat-leaf parsley

*Coeliacs please use gluten-free ingredients

Heat the olive oil in a non-stick frying pan. Finely slice the mushrooms, add them to the pan along with the thyme and sauté them over medium heat until golden and softened. Season the mixture with salt, pepper and grated nutmeg and leave to one side.

Meanwhile, plunge the asparagus into a pan of boiling water and cook them until just tender. Drain the asparagus and keep warm for a few minutes whilst you cut four large circles out of the bread. Use a large pastry cutter or cut round a small coffee cup saucer.

Toast one side of the bread under the grill until golden. Turn the bread over, drizzle with the extra olive oil, brush with a little garlic and finally drizzle with a little truffle oil.

Grill again until the toast is golden.

Arrange the prepared salad leaves on four plates, sprinkle with a little fat-free dressing and place the toasted crostini in the centre.

Quickly heat through the mushrooms for a few seconds and spoon them on top of the toasted crostini. Garnish with the asparagus, a little extra pepper and the parsley. Serve immediately.

Spinach Roulade with Smoked Salmon and Scrambled Eggs

Serves 8 as a starter, 6 as a main course with salads

This roulade is very good either hot in winter or cold in summer, which is when I first tasted it – lapping up the Norfolk sunshine and enjoying delicious food al fresco in the garden.

Roulade

455g/1lb finely chopped frozen spinach
4 large free-range eggs, separated
15g/½ oz reduced-fat butter or margarine-style spread
Sea salt and freshly ground black pepper
A little freshly grated nutmeg
1 tablespoon sesame seeds
Rocket leaves, to garnish (optional)

Filling

115g/4oz smoked salmon
4 large free-range eggs
1 tablespoon filtered water
30g/1oz reduced-fat butter or margarine-style spread
1 standard-sized roulade tin lined with baking parchment

Preheat the oven to 200C/400F/Gas mark 6.

Place the spinach in a non-stick pan with very little water and cook over medium heat until defrosted. Keep stirring and cook the spinach until all the water has evaporated. Remove it from the heat and stir in the egg yolks, butter, salt, pepper and nutmeg.

In a large bowl, beat the egg whites until stiff and then gently fold in the spinach mixture using a metal spoon. Carefully spread the mixture into the prepared tin, sprinkle with half the sesame seeds and bake for about 12–15 minutes until firm to touch.

Meanwhile, prepare the filling. Cut the salmon into little pieces and set aside. Beat the eggs and water together in a bowl and season with salt and pepper. Gently melt the butter and then slowly scramble the eggs in non-stick pan over low heat. They should be slightly runny, as they will carry on cooking as they cool. Leave them to cool completely.

Sprinkle a piece of baking parchment slightly larger than the roulade tin with the remaining sesame seeds and turn out the roulade on to it. Peel off the paper and discard.

Mix the salmon with the cooled scrambled eggs and spread this mixture over the roulade. Roll it up using the sesame-covered paper as a guide and transfer it to a serving plate. Decorate with some rocket leaves and serve or cover the roulade and chill until needed.

Lemon and Caper Stuffed Pears Serves 2

This is a good starter for the summer or an easy and light lunch dish. Choose very ripe pears but make sure that they are not bruised.

2 large, organic, ripe, sweet pears
1 tablespoon lemon juice
15g/½ oz prepared watercress, rocket and spinach salad mix per person
Cold pressed extra virgin olive oil, to drizzle
115g/½ cup virtually fat-free fromage frais
1 tablespoon chopped fresh mint leaves or fresh basil leaves
1 heaped tablespoon capers* in brine, drained
A little chilli sauce* or minced chilli in oil
Sea salt and freshly ground black pepper
A pinch of cayenne pepper

*Coeliacs please use gluten-free ingredients

Peel the pears, cut each one in half, scoop out the core with a teaspoon and then ease out the tough part that runs up to the stalk. Remove the stalk and any bits at the base. Brush the pears with the lemon juice.

Arrange the salad selection on each plate and place two pear halves on each salad. Drizzle the salad with a little oil.

Mix the fromage frais, mint, capers and chilli sauce or minced chilli in a small bowl and season to taste with salt and pepper. Spoon the mixture into the pear cavities, spreading it over the pear flesh to help prevent it from discolouring, then dust with cayenne.

Serve immediately or within the next few hours.

Rocket, Fennel and Strawberry Salad Serves 4

Always eat fresh strawberries at room temperature, as they lose their delicate flavour and natural sweetness when chilled. For sheer extravagance and a romantic dinner for two, you could use *fraises de bois* – cultivated 'wild' strawberries, which are only available at exclusive stores.

Salad

100g/3½ oz fresh, prepared baby rocket leaves
1 large bulb fresh fennel, trimmed and tough outer layers removed
300g/10½ oz fresh strawberries, wiped clean and hulled

Dressing

1 teaspoon crushed coriander seeds
1 teaspoon mild Dijon mustard*
1 tablespoon red wine vinegar
1 small mild red chilli, seeded and finely chopped
Juice of 1 large sweet orange

*Coeliacs please use gluten-free ingredients

Arrange the rocket leaves on each plate.

Using a very sharp knife, cut the fennel in half and then into wafer thin slices. Divide the fennel slices between the salads.

Cut the strawberries into thick slices and arrange them over the salads. (If you do succumb to the temptation of *fraises de bois* then keep the strawberries whole.)

Make the dressing in a small bowl by mixing together the coriander seeds, mustard, vinegar, chilli and orange juice.

Whisk the dressing until it is smooth, drizzle it over the salads and serve.

Avocado and Prawn Salad Serves 6

It may be an old-fashioned combination, but this way is trendy and it's still a winner. As far as I am concerned if a recipe is quick and easy to make, nutritious and popular with everyone, then it is the ideal candidate for a relaxed dinner in the kitchen.

Dressing

60ml/¼ cup cold pressed extra virgin olive oil
250g/1 cup virtually fat-free fromage frais
2 tablespoons tomato ketchup
1 garlic clove, peeled and crushed
2 teaspoons paprika
Sea salt and freshly ground black pepper
A small bunch of chives, finely snipped into small pieces

Salad

A very small handful of prepared mixed lambs lettuce and rocket leaves per person (or any prepared baby leaf mixture)
Juice of 1 lime
3 small ripe avocados
455g/1lb cooked and peeled tiger or jumbo prawns

Place the dressing ingredients in a bowl and, using a fork, mix them together until smooth.

Arrange the salad leaves on 6 small plates.

Squeeze the lime juice into a bowl.

Halve the avocados, remove the stone, quarter, and peel the skin off. Slice the avocado flesh into thick slices and add them to the lime juice. Arrange the avocado slices over the salad and discard any remaining lime juice. Arrange the prawns over the salad and spoon over the dressing. Serve immediately.

You can serve this as a great main course – just treble the amount of salad and it will serve four.

Polenta with Olives and Sweet Peppers Serves 4

Polenta is so versatile I am surprised that we do not use it much in this country. The Italians conjure up divine creamy purees to accompany game or meat and they grill, fry it or bake it smothered in tomato sauce or wild mushrooms. I think it's possible we are really missing a trick here.

500g/1lb 2oz block organic ready-made polenta
4 tablespoons cold pressed extra virgin olive oil
1 garlic clove, peeled and crushed
115g/4oz pitted black olives*
170g/6oz jar pickled sweet baby peppers* (or 1/2 x 375g/13oz jar Peppadew*)
30g/1oz fresh parsley, finely chopped
Freshly ground black pepper
55g/2oz drained anchovy fillets

*Coeliacs please use gluten-free ingredients

Cut the polenta into 8 equal slices. Heat 1 tablespoon of the oil in a non-stick frying pan and fry the polenta slices over high heat until golden and browned on each side. Now add the garlic and cook the polenta on both sides for a further minute. Remove the slices and transfer them to a warm serving plate or dish.

Put the olives, peppers, parsley, black pepper and the remaining oil into a little pan, and briefly heat through.

Meanwhile, arrange the anchovies in a criss-cross pattern over the slices of polenta and then pour over the warm olive, parsley and oil mixture. Serve immediately on its own as a starter, or with lots of salads as a main course.

Smoked Mackerel and Tomato Ramekins Serves 4

Wendy, who is a family friend, very kindly had the whole family over for a fun dinner at New Year when we were staying with my parents in Norfolk. This is her low-fat starter to keep her husband in good shape.

2 fillets (about 200g/6oz) skinned smoked mackerel in crushed peppercorns (for a milder taste use plain smoked mackerel and season with your own quantity of pepper)
12 mini vine tomatoes, halved
250ml/1 cup Elmlea light double cream
A sprinkling of cayenne pepper
4 large ramekins

Preheat the oven to 200C/400F/Gas mark 6.

Break up the mackerel into bite-size pieces and arrange haphazardly with the tomato halves in each ramekin. Pour the cream over the mixture and sprinkle with a dusting of cayenne.

Bake the ramekins for about 20 minutes or until the cream is bubbling, and then serve immediately.

Beetroot Jellies with Celeriac Remoulade Serves 6

Celeriac remoulade is used rather like jumped-up coleslaw. Usually it is made with lashings of olive oil and far more vinegar and mustard than would ordinarily be used in any mayonnaise. This recipe, however, being a fat-free version, has no oil at all.

Beetroot jellies

1 bunch small spring onions, trimmed and sliced
1 teaspoon ground cumin
Sea salt and freshly ground black pepper
140ml/⅔ cup water
140ml/⅔ cup dry white wine
12 small or 8 medium pre-cooked beetroots, peeled and chopped
A few drops of chilli sauce* or minced chilli in oil
1½ sachets/US 1½ tablespoons powdered gelatine, dissolved according to the instructions on the packet, or vegetarian equivalent

Celeriac remoulade

425g/15oz packet fresh, shredded celeriac
Sea salt and freshly ground black pepper
Juice of ½ a lemon
3 tablespoons of Dijon mustard*
2-3 tablespoons boiling water
1 tablespoon wine vinegar
4 heaped tablespoons virtually fat-free fromage frais
2 heaped tablespoons chopped fresh parsley
Some fresh herbs to decorate
6 ramekins or tin moulds, lined on the base with a circle of baking parchment

*Coeliacs please use gluten-free ingredients

Place the spring onions, cumin, salt, pepper, water and wine in a non-stick saucepan and gently cook over medium heat until the onions are nearly soft. Add the beetroot to the pan, heat through and season to taste with chilli sauce or minced chilli. Set aside for 20 minutes. When cool, purée the mixture in a food processor. With the machine still running, add the dissolved gelatine to the purée so that it is evenly distributed.

Fill each of the prepared ramekins or moulds with the purée, cover with clingfilm and chill in the refrigerator for at least 4 hours or until set.

Meanwhile, place the celeriac in a bowl with the remaining remoulade ingredients and mix gently. The sauce should be firm enough to spoon the celeriac into a pile without the sauce running all over the plate. Adjust the seasoning to taste, cover with clingfilm and chill for at least 2 hours or until needed.

Dip the bottom of the moulds into hot water and then loosen the jellies using a sharp knife. Remove the circles of paper. Place a spoonful of the celeriac remoulade beside each jelly and decorate with a few fresh herbs. Serve immediately, or chill until needed.

Spinach and Cheese Moulds Serves 4–6

For special occasions, you can add a few chopped prawns to the cheese filling and then decorate the moulds with whole prawns on a bed of salad leaves. I often change the filling to include pieces of chopped mild red chilli and red pepper.

Cheese moulds

170g/3 cups fresh, young spinach leaves, trimmed
500g/2 generous cups virtually fat-free fromage frais
1 small garlic clove, peeled and crushed
200g/1¼ cups cooked and drained sweetcorn kernels
2 heaped tablespoons shredded fresh basil leaves
Sea salt and freshly ground black pepper
A little freshly grated nutmeg
11.7g sachet/US 1 tablespoon powdered gelatine or vegetarian equivalent, dissolved according to the instructions on the packet

Tomato and red pepper sauce

1 teaspoon ground cumin
400g/14oz can plum tomatoes in natural juice
400g/14oz can pimentos in natural juice, drained
A few drops of chilli sauce* or minced chilli in oil
Sea salt and freshly ground black pepper
Fresh basil leaves or whole baby sweetcorn and fresh rocket leaves, to garnish
4-6 ramekins or tin moulds, lined on the base with a circle of baking parchment

*Coeliacs please use gluten-free ingredients

Cook the spinach in a saucepan with a little water until just wilted. Do not over-cook it, 3 minutes should be enough.

Drain the spinach and pat it dry with absorbent kitchen paper.

Make the sauce. Purée the cumin with the tomatoes and pimentos in a food processor. Add the chilli sauce or minced chilli according to taste and season with salt and pepper. Transfer the sauce to a jug and chill in the refrigerator until needed.

Line the ramekins or moulds with the spinach leaves, covering the base and letting the leaves overhang the edges enough to enable you to fold them back into the middle.

Mix the fromage frais with the garlic, sweetcorn, basil, salt, pepper and nutmeg in a bowl. Stir in the dissolved gelatine, then spoon the mixture into each ramekin and smooth over. Now gently pull the spinach leaves over the filling and cover it with more leaves if necessary, so that there is no filling showing.

Place in the refrigerator for at least 4 hours to set. Loosen the edges of the spinach away from its container and turn each mould out onto the centre of a serving plate. Remove the circle of paper and drizzle the tomato and red pepper sauce over the moulds.

Decorate around the moulds with fresh basil leaves or, for special occasions, place a star of halved baby sweetcorn on each one and serve on a bed of rocket. Serve chilled.

Prawn and Pepper Terrine Serves 8

This terrine is bright and colourful, so there is no need to feel gloomy if you have to give a low-fat dinner party. If you entertain a lot, you can substitute other low-fat seafood or fish, and the peppers can be swapped for any suitable and complementary vegetables.

2 x 22g/¾ oz sachets aspic jelly powder*
900ml/4 scant cups boiling water
100ml/scant ½ cup dry sherry
Sea salt and freshly ground black pepper
A few drops of chilli sauce* or minced chilli in oil
55-85g/¾-1 cup dwarf French green beans, cut into thirds
1 yellow pepper, halved and seeded
1 small bunch of fresh coriander leaves
400g/14oz large peeled prawns, cooked
3 ripe tomatoes, skinned, seeded and cut into eights
Rocket and watercress leaves
A little fresh lemon juice or a good fat-free salad dressing
30.5cm/12in terrine tin

*Coeliacs please use gluten-free ingredients

Dissolve both sachets of aspic jelly powder in a large jug with the boiling water. Add the sherry, seasoning and chilli sauce or minced chilli to taste. Leave the jelly to cool and then transfer it to the refrigerator to thicken it up a little. Keep watching the jelly so that it does not become too thick to handle.

Meanwhile, blanch the green beans in boiling water for 3 minutes, drain and refresh under cold water. Cut the pepper into bite-size pieces. Choose some of the best coriander leaves and set the rest aside to mix in with your salad garnish.

Arrange rows of prawns, green beans, yellow pepper, coriander leaves and tomatoes all the way across and down the length of the terrine tin in any design you like.

Spoon the slightly thickened, cold aspic jelly all over the design until you have a thin, smooth layer covering the seafood and vegetables. Put it in the freezer for a few minutes until set. Repeat this in continuous layers until all the ingredients and jelly are used up. Cover the terrine with clingfilm and chill in the refrigerator until completely firm and set. I suggest at least 4 more hours.

Uncover the terrine. Dip the base of the tin into a basin of boiling water for a second then, using a sharp knife, ease the jelly from around the edges of the tin and quickly turn it onto the centre of an oblong serving dish.

Mix the rocket leaves, watercress and reserved coriander and toss the leaves with a little fresh lemon juice and black pepper (or some really good fat-free salad dressing).

Arrange the salad leaves around the base of the terrine and serve immediately, or keep it in the refrigerator until needed.

Smoked Trout Pâté Serves 6

If you are having this pâté as a starter, you can serve it with wafer thin slices of wheat- or gluten-free toast, some oatcakes or other wheat-free, low-fat crispbreads. Alternatively, you can serve it as a main course on a bed of mixed green salad leaves.

255g/9oz smoked trout fillets or smoked salmon slices
200g/¾ cup virtually fat-free fromage frais
½ teaspoon Dijon mustard*
½ teaspoon creamed horseradish sauce*
A little lemon juice
A little freshly chopped dill
Sea salt and freshly ground black pepper

*Coeliacs please use gluten-free ingredients

Blend the trout with all the remaining ingredients in a food processor and adjust the dill, lemon and seasoning to taste.

Transfer to a serving dish, cover and chill until needed.

The pâté should be soft enough to spread on your toast or crispbreads.

Water Chestnut and Bacon Salad

Makes 20, serves 4 as a starter

These cocktail sticks of bacon-wrapped water chestnuts can be served without the salad and dressing to accompany drinks. If you are having a big party you can easily double, treble or quadruple the ingredients to suit the number of guests. You can prepare them the day before, keep them covered and chilled until just before your guests arrive and then uncover and grill them on a baking tray until crispy.

225g/8oz can whole water chestnuts in water, drained
285g/10oz rindless, smoked, streaky bacon, thinly sliced
A sprinkling of soy sauce*
A drizzle of organic sunflower oil
55g/2oz packet prepared rocket leaves
A sprinkling of bottled or your own fat-free French dressing
20 wooden cocktail sticks

*Coeliacs please use gluten-free ingredients

Wrap each whole chestnut in about one third or half a slice of bacon and secure with a wooden cocktail stick. Arrange them in a baking tray, drizzle with soy sauce and oil and grill them until the bacon is crispy.

Arrange the rocket on four plates and drizzle the leaves with the French dressing. Remove the water chestnuts from the grill and arrange five per person on each bed of rocket. Serve immediately.

fish and seafood

Grilled Scallops with Sage and Capers

Serves 1–2

In Italy, the caper is a delight; large, plump, mellow and juicy – quite unlike the minute offerings we get here in England. The very best capers are grown in Salina, an island off the coast of Sicily. Rather than being drowned in sharp vinegar, they are dried in high quality sea salt, which removes the bitterness and draws out the complex flavours.

255g/9oz scallops, with their corals
6-8 fresh sage leaves, chopped
1 garlic clove, peeled and crushed
Sea salt and freshly ground black pepper
4 tablespoons water
2 heaped tablespoons high quality capers*, rinsed and drained
4 tablespoons Marsala
1 heaped tablespoon chopped fresh parsley

*Coeliacs please use gluten-free ingredients

Place the scallops, sage, garlic, seasoning, water and capers in a non-stick frying pan and cook for about 2–3 minutes. Add the Marsala and cook the scallops for another couple of minutes. Shake the pan from time to time so that the scallops are evenly cooked through.

Remove the scallops from the pan and place on two warm plates. Quickly boil up the juices in the pan for 1–2 minutes. Pour the sauce over the scallops and decorate with a sprinkling of chopped fresh parsley. Serve at once with a mixed green salad with fresh herbs.

Grilled Monkfish with Lentils, Bacon and Fennel

Serves 2

Apart from monkfish, there are few fish that I think combine well with lentils. Thick chunks of salmon, swordfish, tuna or cod are the exception – try these different fish to see which one you prefer.

Fish

1 tablespoon cold pressed extra virgin olive oil
Juice of 1 lemon
A sprinkling of dried flaked or crushed chilli
Sea salt and freshly ground black pepper
1 piece (about 380g/13½ oz) trimmed monkfish tail, skin removed

Lentils

½ x 410g/14½ oz can cooked green lentils (use the rest in a salad for lunch the next day)
½ fennel bulb, trimmed and tough outer layers removed
2 slices dry-cure smoked rindless streaky bacon, finely chopped
1 heaped tablespoon freshly chopped flat-leaf parsley
2 lemon quarters for serving

Preheat the oven to 200C/400F/Gas mark 6.

Mix the oil, lemon juice, chilli, salt and pepper together in an ovenproof dish, add the fish and leave to marinate for about 30 minutes.

Drain and refresh the lentils under cold running water.

Bake the monkfish in the oven for about 20 minutes until opaque and just cooked through.

Meanwhile, finely chop the fennel and fry it with the bacon over medium heat in a non-stick frying pan. The bacon pieces should give off enough fat to stop the fennel sticking but do stir frequently until the bacon is crispy.

Reduce the heat to very low and stir in the lentils. Season with salt and pepper, stir in the parsley, simmer the mixture until the lentils are hot and then keep warm until the fish is cooked.

Take the fish out of the oven and carefully remove the fillets of monkfish from the bone using a sharp knife. Spoon the lentil and bacon mixture onto warm plates, arrange the monkfish at a rakish angle, spoon over any fish juices and serve immediately with the lemon quarters.

Stuffed Squid in Red Wine Sauce Serves 2

Stuffing squid and serving it in a rich sauce is a good way of making this light seafood into a substantial main course. Don't forget that squid needs only brief cooking; otherwise it will become tough and chewy.

2 heaped tablespoons risotto rice
16 whole cleaned squid, with their tentacles
1 small red onion, very finely chopped
2 teaspoons mixed herbs
600ml/2½ cups vegetable or fish stock*
Sea salt and freshly ground black pepper
Freshly grated nutmeg
1 large garlic clove, peeled and crushed
⅓ bottle good Italian red wine
225g/8oz large flat mushrooms
200ml/¾ cup vegetable or fish stock*
100ml/scant ½ cup dry sherry
1 heaped tablespoon tomato purée
1 heaped tablespoon finely chopped sun-dried tomatoes
1 mild chilli, seeded and finely chopped
1 tablespoon wheat-free cornflour*, dissolved in 1 tablespoon cold water
A handful of fresh parsley, finely chopped

*Coeliacs please use gluten-free ingredients

First cook the rice in salted, boiling water until just soft. Drain, rinse under hot water and set aside. Wash the squid in cold water, drain, remove the tentacles and keep in a cool place until needed. Place half the chopped onion, 1 teaspoon of the mixed herbs, the 600ml/2½ cups stock, salt and pepper, nutmeg, garlic and red wine in a large non-stick pan and bring to the boil. Reduce the heat and simmer it until the liquid is reduced by one third.

Chop the mushrooms into fairly large pieces (if using small wild mushrooms keep them whole). Add the mushrooms to the red wine sauce and simmer for about 3 minutes.

Now make the stuffing. Cook the remaining onion in the 200ml/¾ cup of stock and the sherry until soft. Add the cooked rice and the remaining teaspoon of mixed herbs and simmer for a few minutes. Meanwhile, choose six of the smallest squid bodies, finely chop them and add them to the rice along with the tomato purée, sun-dried tomato pieces and chilli. Cook for another 5 minutes or until the squid is just white and the rice is moist but not wet or dry. Adjust the seasoning to taste with salt, pepper and grated nutmeg and remove the rice from the heat. When the rice mixture is cool enough to handle, carefully pack it into each of the squid using your fingertips. Fill the body up, squeeze the mixture down to the end and level it off.

Bring the wine sauce back to simmering point over medium heat, stir in the dissolved cornflour and bring to the boil. Once the sauce has thickened, turn down the heat and place all the stuffed squid and the tentacles in the sauce. Cook the squid over medium heat for a few minutes before turning them over. Simmer only until the squid are cooked through, and then serve them immediately with a sprinkling of fresh parsley. Serve with a delicious continental salad of herbs, mixed lettuce leaves and fresh vine tomatoes.

Spiked Grilled Mahi-Mahi Serves 8

Mahi-mahi is a beautiful blue and gold or green and gold fish that cruises the tropical waters of the world. They are fast growing and, at 35 kilos in 5 years, a mighty big catch on the end of the fishing line. Mahi-mahi is best cooked simply so it's great barbecued or grilled. The quantities in this recipe can be easily halved for four guests.

8 mahi-mahi fillets cut into steaks (choose size according to guests)
2 tablespoons soy sauce*
2 tablespoons cold pressed sunflower oil
2 tablespoons runny honey
½ tablespoon ground ginger
Sea salt and freshly ground black pepper

*Coeliacs please use gluten-free ingredients

Mix the soy sauce, oil, honey, ginger and seasoning together and marinate the fish in the mixture for a few hours. Barbecue or grill the fish under or over very high heat, basting from time to time with the marinade. Serve the fish hot with salads and roasted or barbecued vegetables.

Sardines Napolitana Serves 4–6

Even my husband can make this recipe! He loves fresh sardines and they are so good for us that we try and have them once a week. For a change you can make this with small fresh mackerel – just ask your fishmonger to remove the heads and gut them for you.

700g/1lb 9oz fresh sardines, heads and tails removed, gutted, then washed in cold water
2 tablespoons cold pressed extra virgin olive oil plus a little extra for sprinkling
Sea salt and freshly ground black pepper
2 tablespoons freshly chopped parsley
2 garlic cloves, peeled and crushed
½ tablespoon fresh marjoram
2 x 400g/14oz cans chopped tomatoes
A pinch of cayenne pepper

Preheat oven to 200C/400F/Gas mark 6.

Rinse and dry the sardines then place them in a large, deep ovenproof dish. Mix all the remaining ingredients together and spoon over the sardines. Sprinkle with a little extra oil and cayenne pepper and bake for 20 minutes. Serve hot or cold with a big green salad and a dish of roast peppers or other vegetables.

Tuna Carpaccio with Mint and Caper Salad

Serves 4

It has recently been claimed that eating fresh tuna twice a week has helped some people with stiff joints to feel more mobile. Tuna is an oily fish – which is no doubt why it might help ease stiff joints – but in this recipe the fat content is kept very low by serving it in wafer thin slices with an oil-free dressing. This dish must be ultra fresh otherwise it is not worth making.

2–4 wafer thin slices fresh tuna fillet per person
85g/3oz fresh rocket leaves
Sea salt and freshly ground black pepper
1 mild red chilli, seeded and finely chopped
5 spring onions, trimmed and finely sliced
4 small fresh plum tomatoes, skinned, seeded and finely chopped
1 small cucumber, peeled, halved lengthways and seeded
1 heaped teaspoon Dijon mustard*
2 tablespoons red wine vinegar
½ garlic clove, peeled and crushed
A handful of chopped fresh mint leaves
2 tablespoons good quality capers*, rinsed and drained
Finely grated rind of 1 large unwaxed lemon
Juice of 1 large orange
1 small bunch fresh parsley, chopped

*Coeliacs please use gluten-free ingredients

Ask the fishmonger to slice the tuna into wafer thin slices for you or do it yourself using a very sharp knife. Arrange the rocket leaves on four large plates. Place the tuna slices on the salad leaves and season it all with a little pepper.

In a bowl, mix the chilli with the spring onions and tomatoes and season to taste with salt and pepper. Chop the cucumber into tiny pieces and add to the bowl of tomatoes. Stir in the mustard, followed by the vinegar and garlic.

Now mix in the chopped mint, capers, lemon rind and orange juice and stir gently until it is blended. If you find the dressing too strong, then add a teaspoon of water at a time until the taste is to your liking.

Spoon the salad and juices over the tuna carpaccio and sprinkle with the chopped parsley.

Roast Halibut on Beetroot and Cumin Purée

Serves 2

This lively and colourful dish, full of spices and herbs, reminds me of the Polish soup Borsch. If you use fresh beetroots the flavour will be stronger, but I am normally so busy that I cheat and use ready-cooked and prepared ones instead.

Beetroot and cumin purée

1 large potato, peeled and cubed
2 tablespoons skimmed milk
Sea salt and freshly ground black pepper
4 medium-sized, ready-cooked and prepared beetroot*, not in vinegar
1 fresh garlic clove, peeled and crushed
1 teaspoon wheat-free vegetable stock powder*
½ teaspoon ground cumin
½ teaspoon mixed spice*
250ml/1 cup cold water

Halibut

2 bay leaves
2 freshly prepared halibut steaks (choose size according to appetite)
A large sprig of fresh thyme
Sea salt and freshly ground black pepper
½ a lemon, freshly squeezed
1 lemon, cut into quarters
Fresh thyme sprigs to decorate

*Coeliacs please use gluten-free ingredients

First make the beetroot and cumin purée. Cook the potato in boiling water until soft, then mash with the skimmed milk and season with salt and pepper. Chop the beetroots and put them in a saucepan with the garlic, stock powder, cumin, mixed spice and the cold water. Bring to the boil and simmer for 10 minutes.

Leave the mixture to cool slightly, then purée it in a food processor. (The purée must be very thick otherwise the mash will be too runny to take the weight of the fish. If it is too runny, return it to a non-stick pan and simmer until it has reduced and thickened.)

Mix the beetroot purée into the mashed potatoes and stir the mixture until it is an even texture and colour throughout. Adjust the seasoning according to taste.

Place the beetroot and potato mixture in a non-stick pan and heat through over a gentle heat until needed.

Put the two bay leaves on a non-stick baking tray and place the portions of halibut on top. Sprinkle the fish with the thyme leaves, salt, pepper and some of the lemon juice. Grill the fish for a few minutes under very high heat so that the juices are sealed in. Turn the fish over and grill until just cooked through.

Place the hot purée in the centre of each plate and place the fish on top, removing the bay leaf first. Serve with the lemon quarters and decorate with sprigs of fresh thyme.

Grilled Sea Bass with Orange and Vermouth Sauce

Serves 2

Most sea bass sold in shops has never seen the ocean; like salmon, it is now heavily farmed. Unfortunately, intensively farmed fish have a slightly different texture and taste to wild ones but they are fatter and less expensive which makes them popular.

2 medium-sized (115–170g/4–6oz) sea bass steaks, skin on
Sea salt and freshly ground black pepper
Fresh thyme leaves and a couple of sprigs for decoration
1 fennel bulb, trimmed and tough outer layers removed
Juice of 2 oranges and finely grated rind of 1 unwaxed orange
4 tablespoons extra dry white vermouth
4 tablespoons wheat-free vegetable stock*
5 spring onions, trimmed and finely chopped
1 tablespoon cornflour*, dissolved in 1 tablespoon water

*Coeliacs please use gluten-free ingredients

Rinse the sea bass in cold water and then, using a sharp knife, make 2–3 small incisions on the side of the fish. Put the sea bass on a plate and sprinkle with a little salt, pepper and fresh thyme leaves (reserving a few for decoration). Leave to rest for 30 minutes in a cool place.

Finely slice the fennel with a very sharp knife and place in a non-stick frying pan with the orange juice and rind, the vermouth, stock and spring onions. Bring to the boil, reduce the heat and simmer until the fennel pieces are nearly soft. Stir in the dissolved cornflour, bring the sauce to the boil again, turn down the heat and stir the sauce until it is clear and thickened. Keep the pan of fennel on low heat while you cook the fish.

Preheat the grill to the hottest setting and cook the fish, skin side up, for about 5 minutes. The quicker the fish cooks, the juicier the flesh will be under the seared skin.

Pour the fennel sauce onto two warm plates and place the sea bass in the centre. Decorate with a couple of sprigs of fresh thyme and serve immediately with lots of steamed green vegetables.

Tuna and Chilli Enchiladas Serves 6

Tortillas freeze beautifully, so you can make them in advance, then defrost, fill and bake them for an instant party dish. If you do not like fish, use prawns or chicken instead.

Tortillas

225g/1¾ cups wheat-free flour*, plus extra for kneading and rolling dough
25g/2 tablespoons lard
1 teaspoon fine salt
185ml/¾ cup warm water

Filling

1 tablespoon cold pressed extra virgin olive oil
1 red onion, finely chopped
425g/15oz can chopped tomatoes
1 garlic clove, peeled and crushed
1 teaspoon ground cumin
A freshly chopped chilli (mild, medium or hot according to taste)
1 teaspoon unrefined caster sugar
375g/13oz jar mild or hot baby sweet chilli peppers in spirit vinegar*, drained (Peppadew)
1 tablespoon chopped fresh coriander leaves
455g/1lb fresh tuna

Topping

330ml/1½ cups V8 vegetable juice or tomato juice
170g/1½ cups grated reduced-fat hard cheese or the vegetarian equivalent
A sprinkling of cayenne or sweet paprika

To serve

2 cos lettuce hearts, shredded

2 ripe avocados, stoned and roughly chopped

4 tablespoons chopped fresh coriander

Cold pressed extra virgin olive oil, for drizzling

Sea salt and freshly ground black pepper

500ml/2 cups half-fat crème fraîche or virtually fat-free fromage frais

*Coeliacs please use gluten-free ingredients

Make the tortillas about 2½ hours before you plan to serve the finished dish. Sift the flour into a medium bowl and rub in the lard with your fingertips until it resembles fine breadcrumbs. Make a well in the centre of the mixture. Dissolve the salt in the warm water, and then pour it into the well. Mix with your hands, gradually incorporating the surrounding flour mixture to make a soft dough. Turn this on to a floured board and knead for 2–3 minutes, then place in a floured bowl, cover with clingfilm and leave to rest for 2 hours.

Meanwhile, make the filling. Heat the oil in a frying pan and fry the onions until soft and translucent, but not browned. Stir in the tomatoes, garlic, cumin, chilli and sugar and simmer for about 20 minutes. Add the baby peppers and coriander and simmer for a further 5 minutes whilst you slice the tuna into thin bite-size strips.

Turn the dough out on to a clean and floured surface, knead for 1 minute, and then divide into 12 balls. Keep these covered under clingfilm while you make each tortilla in turn. Flour the surface again and roll out one of the balls to an 18cm/7 inch paper-thin round, giving the dough a quarter turn each time you roll it. Repeat with the remaining dough balls, covering the finished tortillas with clingfilm so that they do not dry out.

Heat a 20cm/8 inch non-stick frying pan over medium-high heat. Add a tortilla and cook for 30–40 seconds until bubbles appear on the surface and the underside is speckled with brown. Do not overcook or the tortilla will be too dry to roll.

Slide the tortilla on to a plate and cover with a piece of baking parchment. Cook the remaining tortillas in the same way, stacking them on the plate with a piece of baking parchment between each.

Preheat the oven to 200C/400F/Gas mark 6.

Spread each tortilla with a very little tomato sauce and arrange a few tuna strips across it. Roll them up and arrange the tortillas in an ovenproof serving dish. Pour the vegetable or tomato juice around the tortillas, sprinkle them with the cheese and add a sprinkling of cayenne or paprika. Bake for about 15 minutes or until the tortillas are bubbling hot and the tuna is just cooked through. Do not over-cook or the tuna will become tough.

Mix the shredded lettuce with the avocado and coriander in a bowl. Drizzle lightly with oil and season with salt and pepper. Serve the enchiladas with a bowl of crème fraîche or fromage frais and accompany them with the lettuce mixture.

Prawn and Ginger Salad Serves 4

This dish is so easy that you can make it in just a few minutes – perfect for a hot summer day when you can't be bothered to cook but have asked friends around.

Dressing

½ sweet red pepper, seeded and finely chopped
½ chilli pepper (mild, medium or hot according to taste), finely chopped
1 tablespoon finely chopped coriander leaves
Sea salt and freshly ground black pepper
1 teaspoon finely grated root ginger
30g/1oz pickled ginger slices in rice vinegar (reserve 2 tablespoons of the rice vinegar)
2 tablespoons cold pressed sunflower oil

Salad

A small handful of rocket per person
455g/1lb cooked jumbo or tiger prawns

Mix all the ingredients for the dressing in a little bowl. Place a small handful of rocket on each plate. Put the prawns in a big bowl, spoon over the dressing and toss them all together. Arrange the prawns and dressing over the rocket and serve.

Grilled Red Mullet with Fennel Seeds and Salsa Verde

Serves 4

Ask your fishmonger to prepare the red mullet for you, or you can do this yourself. Snip off the back and side fins and remove the scales with your hands under cold running water. Now gut the fish, give them a final rinse and dry them on absorbent kitchen paper.

Fish

4 fresh red mullet (choose size according to guests)
2 tablespoons fennel seeds
A drizzle of cold pressed extra virgin olive oil
Sea salt and freshly ground black pepper
Lemon quarters to serve

Salsa Verde

20g/¾ oz flat-leaf parsley leaves
15g/½ oz fresh basil leaves
20g/¾ oz fresh mint leaves
2 garlic cloves, peeled
55g/2oz capers* in wine vinegar
30g/1oz anchovies in oil (drained weight)
1 tablespoon white wine vinegar
4 tablespoons cold pressed extra virgin olive oil
2 teaspoons Dijon mustard*
Freshly ground black pepper

*Coeliacs please use gluten-free ingredients

Rinse the fish under cold running water and pat dry with absorbent kitchen paper. Place the mullet in a baking dish and season them with half the fennel seeds, a drizzle of oil, salt and pepper. Turn them over and repeat the process.

Grill the fish under or over a hot grill for about 4–5 minutes on each side until cooked through.

Meanwhile, put all the salsa verde ingredients in the food processor and whiz briefly until the sauce is reasonably fine but not a purée. Adjust the seasoning if necessary and serve separately. Enjoy the fish with the lemon quarters and plenty of fresh mixed salad.

Sea Bass or John Dory with Sweet Pepper Sauce

Serves 6

Serving a whole fish at dinner is such fun and always looks impressive. It is easy to cook and only takes a few minutes to fillet and serve. You can use any whole fish – John Dory, for example, is delicious even though it is one of the ugliest fish I have seen.

Sweet Pepper Sauce

1 onion, finely chopped
1 tablespoon cold pressed extra virgin olive oil
740g/1lb 10oz ripe tomatoes, quartered
2 teaspoons unrefined caster sugar
1 tablespoon balsamic vinegar
Sea salt and freshly ground black pepper
255g/9oz red peppers, seeded and roughly chopped
250ml/1 cup boiling water

Fish

3 whole, gutted and washed sea bass or 3 John Dory (each fish should serve 2 people, so if you are unsure, ask your fishmonger to judge the correct size for you)
Juice of ½ a lemon
Sea salt and freshly ground black pepper
Rocket and lemon quarters, to garnish

Preheat the oven to 200C/400F/Gas mark 6.

Make the sauce first. In a pan, gently cook the onions in the oil until softened. Add the tomatoes and stir them into the onions. Mix in the sugar, balsamic vinegar, salt and pepper. Simmer for 10 minutes, then add the peppers and water and simmer for 1 hour. Leave the sauce to cool.

Line a deep baking tray with enough foil to enclose all the fish. Rinse each fish under cold water, lay the fish in the tray, sprinkle them with lemon juice, salt and pepper and wrap them together in the foil. Bake the fish in the oven for about 35 minutes depending on size.

Meanwhile, liquidize the cooled sauce and reheat it in the pan.

Remove the fish from the oven and allow them to cool slightly. Now lift them on to a flat dish or clean board and remove the skin. Carefully lift off the fish fillets from the bones and arrange neatly on six warm plates.

Garnish with rocket and lemon quarters and drizzle the fish with a pool of sauce. Serve any remaining sauce in a warm jug.

Crab Tart Serves 4

This is an economical way of using fresh or frozen crab as you only use one for four people. The tart has a fine texture and subtle flavour and is delicious served warm with steamed green vegetables or cold with salads.

Pastry

200g/1½ cups wheat-free flour*
115g/4oz salted butter
1 free-range egg
A little cold water, only if necessary

Filling

1 fresh dressed crab (white and brown meat), discard the shell
4 free-range eggs, beaten
Sea salt and freshly ground black pepper
Freshly grated nutmeg
4 heaped tablespoons half-fat crème fraîche
2 tablespoons finely chopped fresh chives
A dash of chilli sauce* or minced chilli in oil (optional)
1 teaspoon Worcestershire sauce*
1 teaspoon Dijon mustard*

24cm/9½ in fluted loose-bottomed tart tin (if you want to serve the tart cold), lightly greased with reduced-fat butter or margarine and dusted with wheat-free flour* (use a traditional quiche dish for a hot tart)
Ceramic baking beans and baking parchment

*Coeliacs please use gluten-free ingredients

Preheat oven to 190C/375F/Gas mark 5.

Place the flour and butter in a food processor and mix until it resembles breadcrumbs. Add the egg and pulse briefly, just enough so that the dough comes together into a ball. If the mixture is too dry, add a little water. Wrap the dough in clingfilm and chill.

Gently mix all the filling ingredients together in a bowl.

Roll the pastry out into a large enough circle on a clean and floured surface in order to line the prepared tin or quiche dish.

Carefully line the dish, neaten off the edges and prick the base of the pastry with a fork in half a dozen places. Line the pastry with a large circle of baking parchment and fill with ceramic baking beans.

Bake the tart blind for 15 minutes. Remove the tart from the oven and, when cool enough, remove the paper and ceramic beans. Return the pastry to the oven and bake for a further 5 minutes. Remove the tart from the oven and fill it with the crab mixture. Bake the crab tart in the oven for about 20 minutes until the pastry is golden and the filling is set.

When the tart is cold, you can carefully lift it out of the tin, remove the base and then transfer it onto a serving dish. Alternatively, serve the tart straight from the quiche dish.

Seafood Linguine Serves 4–6

Thanks to The Stamp Collection range of wheat-free foods you can enjoy fresh spaghetti. Here it is served in traditional Italian style with lots of garlic, tomato and seafood. The Italians don't approve of serving cheese with seafood pasta, so this is nice and low in fat.

1 red onion, finely chopped
⅓ bottle good quality Italian red wine
340ml/1⅓ cups carrot or vegetable juice
Sea salt and freshly ground black pepper
1 medium or hot red chilli, seeded and finely chopped
400g/14oz can chopped tomatoes
4 bay leaves
1 large sprig fresh oregano
2 large garlic cloves, peeled and crushed
1 teaspoon unrefined soft brown sugar
2 x 250g/9oz packets of The Stamp Collection spaghetti*
Approximately 900g/2lb frozen seafood cocktail, defrosted
A couple of handfuls of fresh basil or fresh parsley leaves, to garnish

*Coeliacs please use gluten-free ingredients

Put the onion, wine, carrot juice, salt, pepper, chilli, tomatoes, bay leaves, oregano, garlic and sugar into a non-stick saucepan and cook over medium heat until the sauce has reduced by about a quarter.

Allow the sauce to cool, remove the bay leaves and liquidize the sauce to a purée. Return the sauce to the pan and adjust the seasoning to taste.

Bring a large pan of salted water to the boil and cook the spaghetti over high heat until al dente. Drain the pasta, refresh under hot water and transfer to a large, warm serving bowl.

Meanwhile, add the seafood to the sauce and simmer for a few minutes until heated through.

Shred the basil leaves or chop up the parsley.

Once again, adjust the seasoning of the seafood sauce and then pour over the waiting pasta. Sprinkle with the herbs and serve.

Fish Pie with Asparagus and Celeriac Serves 4

If you want to be more economical, you can substitute fine green beans for the asparagus – just trim and blanch them before using. You can use any firm white fish for this recipe or, alternatively, smoked haddock or wild salmon.

1 large celeriac, peeled and roughly chopped
2 tablespoons reduced-fat butter or margarine-style spread
Sea salt and freshly ground black pepper
Freshly grated nutmeg
455g/1lb firm white fish fillet, trimmed, skinned and boned
2 tablespoons of wheat-free flour* mixed with 1 tablespoon wheat-free cornflour*
500ml/2 cups skimmed milk
1 teaspoon dried tarragon or a good pinch of fresh tarragon leaves
200g/7oz pack trimmed fresh asparagus tips
A sprinkling of cayenne pepper
30cm/12in wide x 5cm/2in deep ovenproof serving dish

*Coeliacs please use gluten-free ingredients

Preheat the oven to 180C/350F/ Gas mark 4.

Boil the celeriac in a large pan of water until it is soft. Drain the celeriac, allow it to cool and then whiz in the food processor with 1 tablespoon of the butter until you have a smooth purée. Transfer to a bowl, season to taste with salt, pepper and nutmeg and set to one side.

Chop the fish into bite-size pieces and arrange half of it over the base of the dish. Put a pan of water on to boil for the asparagus tips.

Make the tarragon sauce. Melt the remaining tablespoon of butter in a small non-stick pan, but do not boil it, beat in the flour mixture and gradually incorporate the milk. Keep stirring until the sauce boils, then stir in the tarragon and then let it cook for a minute before removing it from the heat. Season to taste with salt, pepper and nutmeg.

Blanch the asparagus for a few minutes until just softened; drain and refresh under running water.

To assemble the fish pie, sprinkle the asparagus over the fish and then top with the remaining fish. Pour over the tarragon sauce and smooth over. Spread the celeriac mash evenly over the fish and sprinkle with cayenne pepper.

Bake in the oven for about 25 minutes or until the fish pie is golden and bubbling.

Seafood Ceviche Serves 4

Beware of drinking and driving – the powerful kick this dish has could take you over the limit! The vodka softens the fish, so it melts in your mouth.

600g/1lb 5oz very fresh or frozen haddock fillets, skinned and boned
1 large mild red chilli, halved and seeded
½ small red onion, finely chopped
170g/6oz very fresh cooked prawns, shells removed
Sea salt and freshly ground black pepper
Juice of 1 large lemon
Finely grated rind and juice of 3 unwaxed limes
4 tablespoons vodka
2 tablespoons chilli olive oil or cold pressed extra virgin olive oil
45g/1½ oz prepared lamb's lettuce
A handful of coriander leaves to garnish

Cut the fish into attractive slender lengths and finely chop the chilli.

Mix the fish and chilli with the onion, prawns, salt and pepper, lemon juice, rind and juice of the limes, vodka and chilli oil in a shallow dish, cover with clingfilm and leave to marinate for 2–4 hours, or overnight.

Arrange the fish salad and all its juices on a serving plate with the lamb's lettuce and sprinkle with a little chopped coriander. Alternatively, serve the salad on individual plates.

meat, poultry and game

Butterflied Lamb with Orange and Parsley

Serves 4–6

Ask your butcher to butterfly a small leg of lamb for you. This term is used because when the meat is laid out in the roasting tin its shape is similar to a butterfly. Basically, the lamb is boned but not rolled and tied.

2 large red onions, very finely sliced
1.3kg/2lb 13oz butterflied leg of lean lamb
A sprinkling dried flaked or crushed chilli
Finely grated rind of ½ an unwaxed orange
Sea salt and freshly ground black pepper
A sprinkling of dried or fresh thyme
1 large garlic clove, peeled and crushed
A drizzle of cold pressed extra virgin olive oil

Preheat the oven to 200C/400F/Gas mark 6.

Lay the onions over the bottom of a large ovenproof dish. Place the lamb, skin side down, over the onions. If it is a tight fit in the tin, squash the meat together to form the shape of a butterfly.

Sprinkle the meat with some chilli flakes, the grated orange rind, some salt and pepper, the thyme and garlic and then drizzle all over a little oil all over the lamb.

Roast the lamb in the oven for about 40 minutes until it is cooked but still pink in the middle.

Remove the lamb from the oven and let it sit for 10 minutes. Carve the meat, arrange the slices with the onions and serve.

Lamb Chops with Funghi Wild

Serves 2

The 'Funghi Wild' brand of dried mushrooms smell particularly earthy and of a damp forest in October. If you're not keen on dried mushrooms you can make this dish with cultivated mushrooms or a mixture of both according to your budget.

4 small lean loin chops (or the tiny cutlets from a rack of lamb)
115g/4oz cultivated mushrooms of any type, wiped clean or trimmed if necessary
30g/1oz good quality dried wild mushrooms
1 tablespoon cold pressed extra virgin olive oil
6 fresh sage leaves or 2 teaspoons chopped dried sage
½ garlic clove, peeled and crushed
1 teaspoon vegetable stock powder*, dissolved in 80ml/⅓ cup boiling water
2 tablespoons Marsala
Sea salt and freshly ground black pepper
1 tablespoon freshly chopped parsley leaves

*Coeliacs please use gluten-free ingredients

Grill the chops under a very hot grill until brown and crispy on each side. Meanwhile sauté both the cultivated and wild mushrooms in the oil with the sage and garlic for a few minutes or until golden and tender. Stir in the prepared stock and simmer for about 3 minutes. Stir in the Marsala, season with salt and pepper and simmer for another 5 minutes.

Spoon the mushrooms and the juices onto the centre of each plate, place the chops across the mushrooms, sprinkle with parsley and serve.

Pork with Tomato and Lemon Serves 4

There are some wonderfully rich Italian regional dishes of wild boar, tomatoes, sage and lemon, all stewed for hours with a bottle of local red wine. Such meals are unbelievably heavy, as you can imagine, and induce a siesta. This is a far lighter version so you won't need a siesta afterwards!

4 thin slices smoked streaky bacon, finely chopped
1 red onion, finely sliced
1 garlic clove, peeled and crushed
60ml/¼ cup good Italian red wine
8 sage leaves, shredded or 2 teaspoons chopped dried sage
Sea salt and freshly ground black pepper
400g/14oz can chopped tomatoes
Finely grated rind of 1 unwaxed lemon
4 lean organic pork steaks or chops, trimmed of any fat
1 tablespoon chopped flat parsley leaves

Preheat the oven to 190C/375F/Gas mark 5.

Dry fry the bacon in a non-stick frying pan for a minute so that the fat is released. Add the onions to the pan and cook until golden and tinged with brown. Stir in the garlic and then the wine and simmer for a moment before adding the sage, salt, pepper, tomatoes and lemon rind.

Arrange the pork steaks or chops in an ovenproof dish and spread the sauce over them. Cover loosely with foil and bake in the oven for about 35 minutes or until the pork is cooked through. The juices should run clear when a skewer is inserted in the centre of the meat. Serve the pork sprinkled with parsley and accompany the dish with plenty of steamed vegetables.

Low-fat Oriental Pork Serves 4

If you love Chinese food but can't go to the local take-away because of wheat intolerance, here is a quick, low-fat and wheat-free recipe that you can serve with stir-fried vegetables.

1 red onion, finely chopped
300ml/1¼ cups water
300ml/1¼ cups vegetable stock*
300ml/1¼ cups unsweetened pineapple juice
Sea salt and freshly ground black pepper
2 tablespoons tomato ketchup
2 small carrots, peeled and cut into matchsticks
1 sweet red pepper, seeded and thinly sliced
1 sweet yellow pepper, seeded and thinly sliced
1 mild or hot red chilli, seeded and thinly sliced
2 garlic cloves, peeled and crushed
1 tablespoon grated root ginger
400g/14oz stir-fry lean organic pork pieces, all visible fat removed
285g/10oz mangetout
2 tablespoons dark soy sauce*
1 tablespoon cornflour*
1 tablespoon wine vinegar
Chopped fresh coriander leaves to decorate

*Coeliacs please use gluten-free ingredients

Put the onion and water in a non-stick frying pan or wok and bring to the boil over high heat. Cook the onion until the water has evaporated, then add the stock and pineapple juice. Season with salt and pepper, stir in the ketchup and add the carrots, peppers, chilli, garlic and root ginger. Cook for 5 minutes, then add the pork, mangetout and soy sauce.

Cook for 3–4 minutes, stirring the ingredients frequently to make sure that they are evenly cooked and coated with the sauce.

Mix the cornflour and vinegar together. Stir this into the mixture and cook until the sauce is thick and clear and coats all the ingredients.

Sprinkle with chopped fresh coriander leaves and serve immediately.

Pork and Olive Casserole Serves 8

When cooking pork, I use lean organic meat and remove any fat I can see. This is a delicious warming winter dish that you can serve with Celeriac Purée (see recipe page 127) and plenty of greens.

900g/2lb baby onions, peeled
2 tablespoons cold pressed extra virgin olive oil
2 garlic cloves, peeled and crushed
Sea salt and freshly ground black pepper
2 teaspoons fresh oregano leaves
2 bay leaves
900g/2lb lean pork, cut into bite-size cubes
1 heaped tablespoon wheat-free cornflour*, dissolved in 2 tablespoons cold water
250ml/1 cup red wine
375ml/1½ cups chicken stock*
A few drops of chilli sauce* or minced chilli in oil
2 heaped tablespoons tomato purée
4 orange peppers, seeded and sliced
400g/14oz pimento-stuffed olives*, drained
2 tablespoons freshly chopped parsley

*Coeliacs please use gluten-free ingredients

Preheat the oven to 180C/350F/Gas mark 4.

In a large flameproof casserole or saucepan cook the onions in the oil until soft and golden. Add the garlic, salt and pepper, oregano, bay leaves and pork and cook until the meat is browned all over. Stir the cornflour, wine, stock, chilli sauce or minced chilli, tomato purée and peppers into the pork.

Cook in the oven for about 1½ hours, then remove and stir in the olives. Return the casserole to the oven to simmer for about 30 minutes. Sprinkle with parsley before serving.

Steak with Lemon and Oil on Rocket Serves 4

You can easily turn this into a special meal for one person – just reduce all the ingredients to a sensible amount and treat yourself to a delicious glass of red wine and a fresh vine tomato and endive salad.

Dressing

2 tablespoons cold pressed extra virgin olive oil
Juice of 1 small or ½ large lemon and the finely grated rind of 1 large or 1½ small unwaxed lemons
2 heaped tablespoons finely chopped parsley

Steaks

4 x 200g/7oz rump, entrecôte, fillet or sirloin steaks
Sea salt and freshly ground black pepper
1 tablespoon cold pressed extra virgin olive oil
1 garlic clove, peeled and crushed
1 handful rocket leaves per person

Combine the dressing ingredients in a bowl and keep to one side.

Season both sides of the steaks with a little salt and pepper and fry them in the oil for a couple of minutes on one side (or longer according to personal preference). Add the garlic and cook the other side until the steaks are nearly ready, then quickly add the dressing and shake the steaks around the pan. After a minute or two remove the steaks, place them on the plates of rocket and drizzle with the dressing.

Liver with Onions and Balsamic Vinegar Serves 2

Liver is wonderfully cheap so we have this once a week – it provides a good dose of vitamin A and is quick to prepare. Serve it with plenty of steamed vegetables or Celeriac Purée (see page 127).

2 tablespoons cold pressed extra virgin olive oil
2 red onions, very finely sliced
8 sage leaves shredded or 2 teaspoons chopped dried sage
1 tablespoon balsamic vinegar
Sea salt and freshly ground black pepper
Freshly grated nutmeg
225g/8oz very finely sliced lambs' liver
60ml/¼ cup Marsala

Heat the oil in a non-stick frying pan, add the onions and fry until they are soft but not browned.

Stir in the sage and the vinegar and simmer until the vinegar has evaporated and the onions are very soft. Season with salt, pepper and nutmeg and then transfer the onions to a warm serving dish.

Quickly fry the slices of liver in the pan until brown on one side, turn them over and add the Marsala. Cook the liver until browned but still pink in the centre. Arrange the liver over the onions, drizzle with any juices and serve immediately.

Smoked Chicken with Caribbean Salad Serves 2–3

I love this easy summer salad. It is plenty for two people and fine for three if you serve it with other salads. For a change you can use other tropical fruit or vegetables instead of the suggested ingredients.

Salad

75g/2½ oz prepared rocket, watercress and baby spinach salad mix
200g/7oz smoked chicken breast on the bone, skinned
¼ cucumber, peeled and thickly sliced
2 ripe kiwi fruit, peeled and thickly sliced
1 small ripe mango, peeled and sliced
¼ small ripe pineapple, peeled, cored and chopped into bite-size pieces

Dressing

1 teaspoon freshly grated root ginger
1 teaspoon runny orange blossom honey
2 teaspoons soy sauce*
1 teaspoon sesame seeds
Juice of ½ an orange
1 tablespoon cold pressed extra virgin olive oil
Freshly ground black pepper

*Coeliacs please use gluten-free ingredients

Arrange the salad leaves on a long serving plate or a big round plate. Carve the chicken thinly and arrange along the length of the plate, or in a circle over the leaves. Arrange the cucumber, kiwi, mango and pineapple around the dish.

Whisk all the dressing ingredients together until amalgamated. Drizzle the dressing all over the salad and serve.

Braised Steak in Port with Cranberry Confit

Serves 4

This is a good hearty casserole and like all meat casseroles benefits from being made the day before and reheated once the flavours have had time to develop. If you have an Aga to cook on, as well as an electric cooker, you can always pop a casserole into the permanently warm oven and let it sit there for hours.

Casserole

2 tablespoons cold pressed extra virgin olive oil
1kg/2¼ lb skirt steak, cut into bite-size pieces
1 large onion, finely chopped
1 large garlic clove, peeled and crushed
1 tablespoon tomato purée
200ml/¾ cup port
425ml/1⅔ cups beef, chicken or vegetable stock*
Sea salt and freshly ground black pepper
1 bouquet garni or 1 tablespoon dried Herbes de Provence
1 heaped tablespoon wheat-free cornflour* dissolved in 2 tablespoons cold water

Confit

1 small red onion, finely chopped
1 tablespoon cold pressed extra virgin olive oil
255g/9oz cranberries (fresh or frozen)
60ml/¼ cup port
1 teaspoon cardamom pods, seeds extracted and pods discarded
Finely grated rind of ½ an unwaxed orange
55g/⅓cup unrefined caster sugar

*Coeliacs please use gluten-free ingredients

Preheat the oven to 160C/325F/Gas mark 3.

Heat 1 tablespoon of the oil in a large flameproof casserole, add the meat and briefly brown it over medium heat. Add the onion and cook until softened but not over browned. Add the garlic and after a few minutes stir in the tomato purée. Add the port, stock, salt, pepper and herbs.

Cover and cook in the oven for about 2 hours, then remove from the heat and stir in the dissolved cornflour. Cover and return to the oven for 30 minutes or until the meat is very tender.

Meanwhile, make the confit. Gently cook the onion in the oil until very soft, making sure it does not brown. Stir in the cranberries, port, cardamom, orange rind and sugar and cook gently for about 15 minutes until thick. Transfer the cranberry confit to a little serving bowl and keep warm.

Remove the casserole from the oven and let it stand for 5 minutes. Serve with the cranberry confit. Celeriac Purée (page 127) is a delicious accompaniment.

Chicken Breasts with Lemon and Lime

Serves 4

I prefer chicken breasts to whole chicken because they are much easier and quicker to cook – and there is no wastage and less fat. Organic chicken is far tastier than those mass-produced chickens generally sold in the supermarket, so it is worth going to your butcher to see what he can procure for you.

4 chicken breast fillets, skinned
Sea salt and freshly ground black pepper
1 tablespoon cold pressed extra virgin olive oil
1 garlic clove, peeled and crushed
200ml/¾ cup extra dry white vermouth
Finely grated rind of ½ an unwaxed lemon
Coarsely grated rind of ½ an unwaxed lime
340g/12oz fresh spinach, washed and dried
A sprinkling of freshly grated nutmeg

Season the chicken breasts with salt and pepper. Heat the oil in a big non-stick frying pan and saute the chicken breasts in the oil until golden and slightly browned on one side. Turn the breasts over, reduce the heat, add the garlic and cook until just tinged with golden brown.

Drain off any excess oil from the pan and reduce the heat further. Stir in the vermouth and add the grated lemon and lime. Simmer for about 10 minutes until the chicken is cooked.

Cook the spinach for a couple of minutes in a pan of boiling water, drain and season with salt, pepper and nutmeg. Arrange the spinach on a flat warm serving dish and keep warm. Lift out the chicken breasts with a slotted spoon and arrange them on the bed of spinach. Increase the heat to high and boil the sauce until reduced by half. Spoon the sauce over the chicken and serve.

Sticky Ginger Chicken Kebabs Serves 2

You can buy the wooden skewers used in this recipe in supermarkets and kitchen shops. If you soak them in cold water for 10 minutes before using, they won't become charred. I also use them for fruit kebabs in the summer.

½ red onion, cut into quarters
1 teaspoon orange juice
2 teaspoons sesame seeds
1 tablespoon unrefined natural molasses sugar
1 teaspoon freshly grated root ginger
5 cardamom pods, split and seeds extracted
1 teaspoon dark soy sauce*
A sprinkling of dried flaked or crushed chilli (optional)
Freshly ground black pepper
2 skinned chicken breasts, trimmed of fat and cut into bite-size pieces

*Coeliacs please use gluten-free ingredients

Blanch the onion quarters in a small pan of boiling water for 3 minutes until softened. Drain and refresh under cold running water and leave to drain on a double layer of absorbent kitchen paper.

In a bowl, mix the orange juice, sesame seeds, sugar, ginger, cardamom seeds, soy sauce, chilli flakes and pepper. Mix in the chicken pieces, coating evenly. With clean hands, slip pieces of chicken and bits of onion alternately along the skewers.

Grill or barbecue the kebabs under or over high heat until golden and cooked through (check this by inserting a sharp pointed knife into the chicken and if the juices run clear the meat is cooked). Serve the kebabs on a bed of salad.

Raj Chicken Serves 6

The sauce used in this recipe is marvellous because it is just as perfect spooned over pheasant breasts or smoked chicken breasts. I often use it for hot buffets, served with plenty of roasted vegetables and salads.

6 cooked, skinned chicken breasts
280ml/1⅓ cups Elmlea light double cream
2 tablespoons Worcestershire sauce*
2 tablespoons mango chutney*
Sea salt and freshly ground black pepper

*Coeliacs please use gluten-free ingredients

Preheat the oven to 200C/400F/Gas mark 6.

Arrange the chicken breasts in a deep ovenproof serving dish (as the cream melts it will overflow if the dish is too shallow).

In a mixing bowl, whip the cream until it forms soft peaks, then stir in the Worcestershire sauce, chutney, salt and pepper. Spoon the sauce over the chicken and bake for about 15-20 minutes until browned and bubbling.

Serve hot with plenty of steamed fresh vegetables.

Quail and Grape Salad Serves 4

If you don't like quail or if you have already made this recipe several times, you may like to make it with petit poussins instead. It will be just as delicious and impressive.

4 prepared oven-ready quail
A drizzle of cold pressed extra virgin olive oil
Sea salt and freshly ground black pepper
1 teaspoon fresh thyme leaves
125ml/½ cup white wine
140g/5oz seedless red grapes
85g/3oz prepared watercress, rocket and baby spinach salad mix
Extra cold pressed extra virgin olive oil and balsamic vinegar

Preheat the oven to 200C/400F/Gas mark 6.

Place the quail in an ovenproof dish. Drizzle with the oil and season with the salt, pepper and thyme. Add the wine to the dish and roast the quail until cooked but still pink – this will take about 25 minutes. Let the quail rest for 5 minutes.

Cut the grapes into halves. Arrange the salad leaves on four plates and arrange the grapes over the salad leaves.

Add some extra oil and balsamic vinegar to the juices in the roasting dish, whisk briefly and taste to check that you have got the balance right. Pour this dressing over each salad. Place a quail on each salad and serve immediately.

Chicken Galantine with Green Peppercorns

Serves 8

Ask your butcher to bone the chicken for you or if you know how to bone a chicken you can do this yourself – it is worth all the effort to end up with this classic French dish. I love making it in summer and serving it cold the next day with lots of salads.

You can easily wrap it up and carve it at picnics or at an al fresco lunch, when it is particularly delicious with a tomato and basil salad.

1.8kg/4lb fresh free-range chicken
100g/3½ oz prosciutto, thinly sliced
340g/12oz lean minced pork
200ml/¾ cup half-fat crème fraîche
Sea salt and freshly ground black pepper
Freshly grated nutmeg
2 tablespoons green peppercorns* in brine
A little cold pressed extra virgin olive oil
Watercress, rocket and baby spinach prepared salad mix, to garnish (optional)

*Coeliacs please use gluten-free ingredients

Preheat the oven to 190C/375F/Gas mark 5.

Bone the chicken with a very sharp knife. Spread the chicken on a clean board, skin side down, and cover the meat with the strips of prosciutto.

Mix the pork, crème fraîche, salt, pepper, nutmeg, green peppercorns and any leftover chicken pieces (from the boning) in a bowl. Spread this mixture over the prosciutto. Bring up each side of the chicken so that they meet in the centre and overlap. Brush the skin with a little oil, then lay the chicken on a large piece of foil. Push any oozing stuffing back in at the ends and wrap up the chicken as tightly as possible in the foil, forming a giant sausage shape.

Chill the chicken for 30 minutes on a baking tray in the refrigerator.

Transfer the chicken to the oven and roast it in its foil on the baking tray for about 1 hour, or until the juices run clear when a skewer is inserted into the meat.

When you remove the chicken from the oven, transfer it to a flat dish, but you must keep it in the foil for a couple of hours. When it is cool enough, transfer it to the refrigerator. Chill for a few hours or overnight before unwrapping it and carving. Serve the chicken in its own jelly, decorated with the optional prepared salad.

We had this recipe hot one night for a dinner party and it was absolutely delicious. Just let the chicken cool a little for 15 minutes still wrapped in the foil, then unwrap it and carve. Reheat the juices gently whilst you are carving and drizzle the warmed juices over each serving.

Sweet Duck with Courgettes, Mangetout and Sesame Seeds Serves 2

Mass produced duck can be tasteless and fatty, so try to buy organic, or at least a top quality bird. Like all stir-fries, this recipe is quick, easy and delicious, as well as low-fat and infused with oriental flavours. You can also make this recipe with chicken or turkey.

Sauce

2 tablespoons reduced-sugar marmalade
1 tablespoon soy sauce*
A few drops chilli sauce* or minced chilli in oil
Freshly ground black pepper
1 teaspoon wheat-free cornflour*
1 teaspoon organic rice wine vinegar
1 teaspoon freshly grated root ginger
½ garlic clove, peeled and crushed

200g/7oz dwarf courgettes
200g/7oz mangetout or sugar snap peas
2 duck breasts (about 400g/14oz in total) with skin on
1 tablespoon sesame seeds
1 tablespoon freshly chopped coriander leaves

*Coeliacs please use gluten-free ingredients

Mix the marmalade, soy sauce, chilli, pepper, cornflour, rice wine vinegar, ginger and garlic together in a bowl and set aside.

Bring a pan of water to the boil. Meanwhile, cut the courgettes in half lengthwise and cut each mangetout in half lengthwise. Plunge the courgettes into the boiling water, cook for 2 minutes then add the mangetout and cook for a further minute. Drain the vegetables.

Dry-fry the duck breasts skin-side down in a non-stick frying pan until the skins are dark brown and crispy. Turn them over and cook the meat so that it is browned on the outside but still very pink inside.

Remove the duck from the pan and leave it on a clean board for a moment. When the duck is cool enough, cut off the skin using a sharp knife and discard it. Meanwhile, add the sauce mixture and the vegetables to a wok and stir-fry over high heat until the sauce becomes shiny and thick. Quickly slice the duck meat into diagonal slices, add to the stir-fry and toss for a minute or two. Sprinkle with the sesame seeds and the coriander and serve immediately.

Guinea Fowl with Port and Orange Serves 4

Guinea fowl can now be bought in most large supermarkets, but if it's not available you can make this recipe with chicken or pheasant. Serve this dish with Celeriac Purée (see page 127) and plenty of steamed green vegetables.

1 guinea fowl (about 1kg/2¼ lb)
A little cold pressed extra virgin olive oil
1 small onion, finely chopped
55g/2oz finely cubed rindless bacon or pancetta pieces
1 garlic clove, peeled and crushed
125ml/½ cup port
300ml/1¼ cups chicken stock*
1 tablespoon redcurrant jelly
Coarsely grated rind of ½ an unwaxed orange
1 bay leaf
Sea salt and freshly ground black pepper
1 heaped tablespoon wheat-free cornflour* dissolved in 2 tablespoons cold water

*Coeliacs please use gluten-free ingredients

Preheat the oven to 190C/375F/Gas mark 5 (or use the hob).

Joint the guinea fowl into 4 portions, either 2 breasts and 2 legs or ½ a breast each with a leg and thigh joint each.

Warm a little oil in a large frying pan or flameproof casserole and brown the joints until golden. Transfer them to a plate. Add the onion and bacon to the pan, cook for about 3 minutes and add the garlic. Add the port and simmer for a couple of minutes. Add the stock, jelly, orange rind, bay leaf, salt and pepper, and return the guinea fowl to the simmering pan.

Cover with a lid and cook on a low temperature for about 40 minutes or, if using a casserole, cook in the oven for about the same amount of time.

When the guinea fowl is cooked, stir in the dissolved cornflour and water and simmer over medium heat until the sauce thickens. (Alternatively, return the casserole to the oven and cook for a further 10 minutes in order to thicken the sauce).

Let the guinea fowl rest for a few minutes before serving.

Turkey Loaf with Bean and Lime Salsa Serves 6

Broad beans are full of vitamin C, iron and fibre. Choose the youngest and greenest beans for the sweetest flavour and do not over-cook or they will discolour and wrinkle.

Loaf

2–3 large courgettes
1 onion, finely chopped
2 large garlic cloves, peeled and crushed
900g/2lb lean turkey meat, minced
2 heaped tablespoons chopped fresh parsley
2 heaped tablespoons chopped fresh chives
1 tablespoon chopped fresh rosemary
1 large free-range egg white, lightly beaten
Sea salt and freshly ground black pepper

Salsa

455g/1lb frozen baby broad beans
1 tablespoon unrefined dark brown sugar
425g/15oz can chopped tomatoes
1 red chilli, seeded and finely chopped
½ red onion, finely chopped
Finely grated rind and juice of 1 fresh unwaxed lime
A large handful of fresh basil leaves, torn into small pieces
A large handful of fresh parsley leaves, finely chopped
Sea salt and freshly ground black pepper

30cm/12in non-stick terrine tin, lined with baking parchment

Preheat the oven to 190C/375F/Gas mark 5.

Trim the courgettes and cut them into thin ribbons using a vegetable peeler or a hand-held metal cheese slicer. Bring a saucepan of water to the boil, add the courgettes and blanch over high heat for 1 minute. Drain and rinse under cold water.

Line the prepared tin with the courgettes, going from side to side and ensuring that they touch each other. Cover the ends of the terrine tin with some more slices, making sure that they overlap enough to prevent gaps.

Put the onion, garlic and minced turkey in a bowl with all the herbs and beaten egg white and combine it thoroughly. Season with salt and pepper. Place half the turkey mixture into the prepared base of the tin and level it off. Cover the mixture with any leftover courgette slices. Now cover the courgettes with the remaining turkey mixture. Press it all firmly down and then cover with a very thick layer of baking parchment.

Set the terrine tin in a baking tray with enough water to come a third of the way up the side of the terrine tin. Place the tray in the oven and bake for 1½ hours until the loaf is cooked through. (The terrine is ready when an inserted skewer comes out clean and the juices are clear.)

Meanwhile, make the salsa. Cook the broad beans in boiling water for about 5 minutes until tender. Drain them and refresh under cold water. When the beans are cool enough to touch, peel off the skins and discard them. Put the beans in a bowl, mix in all the remaining salsa ingredients and season to taste with salt and pepper. Chill the mixture until the turkey loaf is ready.

When the turkey loaf is cooked through, cool slightly so that you can remove the paper and turn it out onto a serving dish. Peel off the remaining paper and serve the loaf hot with the chilled bean and lime salsa.

vegetarian main courses

Chickpea Salad with Peppers and Tomatoes

Serves 4

This is an easy salad to take for lunch at work or on a picnic. It is also delicious with other salads and baked potatoes in winter or boiled new potatoes in summer.

400g/14oz can chickpeas, drained
400g/14oz can Italian cherry tomatoes, drained
1 sweet red pepper, seeded and finely sliced
1 tablespoon finely chopped fresh mint
1 tablespoon finely chopped coriander
1 tablespoon finely chopped parsley
2 tablespoons fresh lime juice
2 tablespoons cold pressed extra virgin olive oil
Sea salt and freshly ground black pepper
A sprinkling of dried flaked or crushed chilli
½ garlic clove, peeled and crushed

Put all the ingredients in a bowl and toss until evenly coated. Transfer the salad to a bowl and serve with other salads or hot potatoes. Alternatively, pack half of the salad in an airtight container for lunch, and cover and chill the remainder for the following day.

Savoy Pasta   Serves 2

This is a very good way of sneaking some cabbage into the diet. I particularly love Savoy cabbage as it has such a delicate taste. When the cabbage is cut into wafer thin slices it only needs blanching in boiling water for a few seconds.

115g/4oz gluten-free corn penne
30g/1oz reduced-fat hard cheese, finely grated (optional)
Sea salt and freshly ground black pepper
Freshly grated nutmeg
About half a small Savoy cabbage (once the outer leaves and base have been removed), very thinly sliced
2 tablespoons cold pressed extra virgin olive oil
1 small garlic clove, peeled and crushed
A dash of minced chilli in oil
15g/½ oz fresh basil leaves, finely shredded

Cook the pasta until al dente in a pan of boiling water. Drain and refresh it briefly under running water. Return the pasta to the pan, stir in the cheese (if using), season with salt, pepper and nutmeg and cover to keep warm.

Meanwhile, blanch the cabbage in a pan of boiling water for a few seconds – up to a minute – and then drain and stir into the pasta.

In a small saucepan, briefly heat the oil with the garlic and chilli then drizzle it over the pasta and toss gently. Transfer the pasta to a warm serving bowl and sprinkle with the basil. Serve immediately with plenty of mixed salad.

Lentil Salad with Artichokes and Peppers

Serves 4 or makes 2 lunches

Here is another easy salad which can be quickly whisked up. It's great for your lunch box, or enjoyed with other salads and baked potatoes in winter or boiled new potatoes in summer.

400g/14oz can green lentils, drained
400g/14oz can artichoke hearts, drained and halved
400g/14oz can whole sweet pimentos, drained and thinly sliced
Sea salt and freshly ground black pepper
1 tablespoon chopped fresh basil leaves
1 tablespoon chopped fresh chives
1 tablespoon chopped fresh parsley
2 tablespoons lemon juice
2 tablespoons cold pressed extra virgin olive oil

Mix all the ingredients together in a bowl and toss to coat evenly. Transfer the lentil salad to a serving bowl and serve with other salads and hot potatoes. Alternatively, pack half in an airtight container for lunch, and cover and chill the remainder of the lentil salad for the following day.

Vegetable Goulash Serves 4

We always have three vegetarian dinners each week so that we give our digestive systems a chance to recover from the arduous task of digesting red meat – and as a break from fish and seafood. This dish is warming and filling, which is ideal in the winter.

2 tablespoons cold pressed extra virgin olive oil
1 large red onion, finely sliced
2 sweet red peppers, halved and seeded
2 garlic cloves, peeled and crushed
1 teaspoon cumin seeds
1 teaspoon caraway seeds
2 heaped teaspoons sweet paprika
2 large organic carrots, peeled and cut into batons
2 large sweet potatoes, peeled and cut into bite-size pieces
500ml/2 cups carrot juice
425ml/1⅔ cups vegetable stock*
2 tablespoons tomato purée
Chilli sauce* or minced chilli in oil according to taste
Sea salt and freshly ground black pepper
2 bay leaves
400g/14oz can red kidney beans, drained
Virtually fat-free fromage frais, to serve (optional)

*Coeliacs please use gluten-free ingredients

Heat the oil in a flameproof casserole, add the onions and cook over medium heat until golden. Meanwhile, grill the pepper halves until the skins are charred and blistered. Allow the peppers to cool, then peel off the skins with a sharp knife and discard. Cut each pepper half into four and keep to one side until needed.

Stir the garlic, all the spices, carrots and potatoes into the casserole and cook for a couple of minutes. Add the carrot juice and stock and stir in the tomato purée, chilli, salt, pepper and bay leaves. Simmer with the lid on for about 25 minutes, stirring occasionally to prevent the goulash from sticking to the casserole.

Add the peppers and kidney beans and continue to cook for a further 25 minutes.

Spoon a dollop of fromage frais on top of each plate of goulash and serve with bowl of steamed brown rice.

Wild Mushrooms with Lentils Provençal

Serves 4

Autumn walks in the woods, with glorious coloured leaves and crisp, clean air is to me one of the marvels of nature. Nestling under the leaves and around the huge old trees bloom delicious wild mushrooms to be collected along the way. This lovely French recipe can be used with any safe fresh or dried mushrooms of your choice.

1 litre/4 cups water
1 large red onion, thinly sliced
255g/9oz Puy or green lentils
250ml/1 cup sweet red vermouth
1 tablespoon vegetable stock powder*
Sea salt and freshly ground black pepper
Freshly grated nutmeg
3 sprigs fresh rosemary
45g/1½ oz dried, mixed wild mushrooms (or any quantity of fresh ones)

*Coeliacs please use gluten-free ingredients

Boil the water in a non-stick pan, add the onion and cook for about 10 minutes. Add the lentils and continue cooking over medium-high heat for another 10 minutes, stirring from time to time. (If the liquid reduces too much, add some more water.)

Pour in the vermouth and cook for 5 minutes. Now stir in the stock powder, salt, pepper, nutmeg and rosemary, reduce the heat and simmer for 15 minutes.

Finally, mix in the mushrooms and leave the pot to simmer for about 20 minutes.

Adjust the seasoning and serve with warm wheat-free bread and a fresh green salad.

Thai Vegetable Curry Serves 6

I have been hooked on Thai and Malaysian food since my friend Sarah and I went round Thailand, Sri Lanka, Malaysia and the Philippines for an eight-week foodie tour – combined, of course, with lying on idyllic beaches and endless whizzing in and out of glorious temples and beautiful gardens.

1 tablespoon organic sunflower oil
1 large onion, finely sliced
4 teaspoons Thai green curry paste*
500ml/2 cups vegetable stock*
½ butternut squash, peeled, seeds and pith removed
1½ x 400ml/14oz cans reduced-fat coconut milk
200g/7oz courgettes, thickly sliced
200g/7oz carrots, cut into matchsticks
155g/5½ oz broccoli, cut into bite-size florets
155g/5½ oz cauliflower, cut into bite-size florets
75g/2½ oz sugar snaps or mangetout
½ mild green chilli, seeded and roughly chopped
1 garlic clove, peeled and crushed
15g/½ oz fresh basil leaves

*Coeliacs please use gluten-free ingredients

Heat the oil in a large deep frying pan or wok, add the onion and curry paste and cook for 4–5 minutes over medium heat. Add the stock and the squash and cook over medium heat until the squash has considerably softened.

Stir in the coconut milk, all the other vegetables, chilli and garlic and simmer at bubbling point until the vegetables are tender and the sauce has reduced.

Serve the curry sprinkled with the basil leaves and accompany with a bowl of steamed fragrant Thai rice.

Saffron, Pea and Sun Blush Tomato Risotto

Serves 3 as a main course or 4 as a starter

Risotto should be cooked slowly so that it becomes creamy and rich without the need to add butter, cream or cheese. This is a very easy and versatile vegetarian risotto – you can change the peas to baby broad beans and the tomatoes to pickled sweet red peppers*.

1 tablespoon cold pressed extra virgin olive oil
1 onion, finely chopped
170g/6oz Arborio rice
125ml/½ cup white wine
2 heaped teaspoons vegetable stock powder *
Finely grated rind of 1 unwaxed lemon
1 teaspoon fresh thyme leaves
A good pinch of saffron
115g/4oz frozen peas
140g/5oz tub sun blush tomatoes in oil (available from the deli counter)
Sea salt and freshly ground black pepper
A handful of fresh basil leaves, roughly chopped

*Coeliacs please use gluten-free ingredients

Heat the oil in a medium-sized pan, add the onions and cook gently in the oil. Don't let the onions brown. When they are nearly soft, stir in the rice and cook for about 1 minute before adding the wine, stock powder, lemon rind and thyme. Let the rice simmer until the wine has been absorbed, then ladle in 250ml/1 cup of water and stir in the saffron.

Stir the rice from time to time and top up with another cup of water before the rice starts to stick. Keep going until the rice is creamy and soft (you will probably need another cup of water).

Meanwhile, cook the peas in boiling water, drain and keep them warm.

When the risotto is cooked, gently stir the peas into the rice. Using clean fingers, lift the tomatoes out of the oil and into the rice (this will provide just the right amount of oil to make the rice sleek and glossy, so discard the remaining oil if it is more than a teaspoonful). Season the rice to taste with salt and pepper and sprinkle with the chopped basil.

Serve the risotto immediately accompanied by a big salad of your favourite salad leaves, for instance rocket, watercress, chicory and spinach.

Carrot Risotto with Chermoula

Serves 4

Chermoula is a spicy Moroccan sauce or marinade that is often eaten with fish or seafood. Here it is pungent foil for this subtle risotto. You can serve it with a big salad of mixed leaves and herbs, a dish of vine tomatoes and fresh basil or a plate of roasted red and yellow peppers.

Chermoula

2 large garlic cloves, peeled
30g/1oz fresh coriander leaves
20g/¾ oz fresh mint leaves
30g/1oz fresh basil leaves
1 teaspoon ground cumin
1 teaspoon ground paprika
Some minced chilli in oil or chilli sauce*
6 tablespoons cold pressed extra virgin olive oil
Juice of 1 lemon

Risotto

1 onion, finely sliced
1 litre/4 cups strong vegetable stock*
2 garlic cloves, peeled and crushed
200g/1 cup risotto rice
4 tablespoons white wine
Finely grated rind and juice of 1 unwaxed lemon
455g/1lb organic carrots, peeled and coarsely grated
Sea salt and freshly ground black pepper

*Coeliacs please use gluten-free ingredients

Blend the Chermoula ingredients in a food processor until they become a fine sauce but not a purée, then transfer the sauce to a little bowl.

Now make the risotto. Cook the onions in the stock until soft and about half of the liquid has evaporated. Stir in the garlic and rice and cook for a minute before adding the wine. Stir in the lemon rind and let the rice simmer gently, stirring frequently, until the rice is soft and plump. Add more water if necessary to prevent the rice from sticking.

Lastly, stir in the grated carrots, lemon juice, salt and pepper and let it warm through.

Pile the risotto onto a warm serving dish and top with the Chermoula.

Spaghetti with Lemon and Courgettes Serves 2

Most seasonal green vegetables work well in this instant lunch or supper recipe. Sometimes, if there are not any courgettes around, I use frozen baby broad beans.

115g/4oz fresh wheat-free spaghetti* (or dried gluten-free)
2 medium-sized firm courgettes, finely sliced
2 tablespoons cold pressed extra virgin olive oil
Juice and finely grated rind of ½ an unwaxed lemon
A sprinkling of dried flaked or crushed chilli
½ garlic clove, peeled and crushed
Sea salt and freshly ground black pepper
1 tablespoon freshly chopped parsley leaves
30g/1oz reduced-fat hard cheese, grated (optional)

*Coeliacs please use gluten-free ingredients

Bring a pan of water to boil for the spaghetti and another one for the courgettes. Cook the spaghetti in salted boiling water until *al dente*. At this point plunge the courgettes into the boiling water to cook until just tender.

Drain and then refresh the pasta briefly under running water. Return the spaghetti to the pan and toss in the oil, lemon juice and rind, chilli, garlic, salt, pepper and parsley.

Drain the courgettes and transfer to a warm pasta bowl. Mix in the spaghetti and oil mixture and serve immediately with or without grated cheese.

Macaroni Cheese Serves 2

This is another super-quick recipe for emergencies or just when you don't feel like cooking!

You can make the recipe with your favourite shape of pasta but don't use spaghetti or tagliatelle. You can also make it less calorific by substituting half the crème fraîche for virtually fat-free fromage frais.

125g/4½ oz corn penne or other wheat-free* pasta shapes
500ml/2 cups half-fat crème fraîche (or 50% quantity of virtually fat-free fromage frais)
1 teaspoon Worcestershire sauce*
1 teaspoon Dijon mustard*
Sea salt and freshly ground black pepper
55g/2oz reduced-fat hard cheese, grated
A pinch of cayenne pepper

*Coeliacs please use gluten-free ingredients

Preheat the oven to 200C/400F/Gas mark 6.

Bring a pan of water to the boil and cook the pasta until *al dente*. Drain the pasta and refresh under running water. Spread the pasta over the base of a small ovenproof baking dish.

In a bowl, mix the crème fraîche with the Worcestershire sauce, Dijon mustard, salt, pepper and half the cheese, then spread it over the top of the pasta. Sprinkle the pasta with the remaining cheese and a little cayenne.

Bake the macaroni cheese in the oven for about 15 minutes until the cheese is bubbling and golden. Serve immediately with salad or steamed greens.

Low-Fat Creamy Pasta

Serves 3

I made this pasta dish recently for some American friends of mine who do not eat any fat and are vegetarians. They didn't realize that the fresh pasta I used was gluten-free, so that I could indulge too!

1 red onion, roughly chopped
250ml/1 cup water
100ml/scant ½ cup red wine
1 plump garlic clove, peeled and crushed
3 stalks fresh thyme
2 bay leaves
250ml/1 cup carrot or vegetable juice
1 chilli, seeded and chopped
4 tablespoons 100% natural pumpkin purée
1 tablespoon wheat-free cornflour* dissolved in 1 tablespoon water
Sea salt and freshly ground black pepper
Freshly grated nutmeg
255g/9oz packet of The Stamp Collection wheat-free fresh spaghetti* or other dried varieties available
4-5 tablespoons virtually fat-free fromage frais or set plain Greek yogurt
A little freshly chopped parsley and/or grated reduced-fat pecorino cheese

*Coeliacs please use gluten-free ingredients

Place the chopped onion in a non-stick pan, add the water and bring to the boil. Drain the onions and refresh them under cold water. Return the onions to the pan with the same amount of fresh water as before and bring to the boil once again.

This time, cook the onions until all the water evaporates. Add the wine, garlic, thyme and bay leaves to the pan and, stirring frequently, cook for 3-5 minutes until the wine reduces.

Now stir in the carrot juice and chilli and simmer for another 5 minutes. Stir in the pumpkin purée, followed by the dissolved cornflour and cook for a few minutes. Reduce the heat to low, season to taste with salt, pepper and nutmeg and let the sauce simmer gently while you cook the pasta.

Cook the spaghetti in boiling water for a couple of minutes. Drain the pasta, refresh under hot water and then return it to the saucepan. Cover with fresh water, bring to the boil again and cook until *al dente*. This prevents the spaghetti becoming sticky and heavy.

Increase the heat slightly under the sauce, add the fromage frais or yogurt to the pan and let it simmer for a couple of minutes, stirring frequently (do not let it boil or the sauce might separate). Drain the cooked spaghetti and transfer it to a warm serving bowl. Pour the hot sauce over the spaghetti and serve immediately, sprinkled with either the chopped parsley or grated pecorino or both.

Sweet Pepper and Courgette Risotto

Serves 8

Courgettes have a high water content and are low in calories. They should always be firm and shiny, not dull and floppy. The bigger the courgette the less flavour it has, so choose small ones, though not the dwarf variety.

1 large red onion, finely chopped
½ bottle Italian white wine
2 large sweet red peppers, seeded and coarsely chopped
2 large courgettes, cut diagonally
170g/6oz of your favourite mushrooms, thickly sliced
1 large sprig thyme
1 large sprig rosemary
4 bay leaves
2 garlic cloves, peeled and crushed
Sea salt and freshly ground black pepper
1 red chilli, seeded and finely chopped
1 tablespoon vegetable stock powder*
115g/⅔ cup Italian risotto rice
340ml/1⅓ cups carrot juice
A pinch of saffron
A large handful of fresh basil leaves, shredded

*Coeliacs please use gluten-free ingredients

Place the onion and wine in a large, non-stick pan and cook over medium heat until the onion softens. Top up with water if the liquid evaporates too quickly.

Add the peppers, courgettes, mushrooms, all the herbs, garlic, salt and pepper and chilli. Cook for about 5 minutes, then add the stock powder, rice, carrot juice, saffron and 600ml/ 2½ cups of hot water. Simmer the risotto for about 15 minutes, until most of the liquid is absorbed, then top up with about half again of hot water (different kinds of rice absorb liquids differently, so the amount of water you will need to keep the rice moist will vary).

Simmer the rice and vegetables for another 15 minutes until they are tender. Adjust the seasoning to taste, adding more chilli if you like your risotto highly seasoned. Stir the risotto from time to time, to prevent it sticking to the bottom of the pan.

Serve the risotto in a warm dish and sprinkle liberally with shredded basil leaves and black pepper.

vegetables

Mushroom and Pak Choi Stir-fry Serves 4

This Chinese dish goes very well with a bowl of instant 100% rice noodles or a bowl of steamed Fragrant Thai rice and other stir-fries or low-fat vegetarian dishes.

1 tablespoon dark soy sauce*
2 tablespoons rice wine
1 teaspoon wheat-free cornflour*
1 teaspoon runny honey
1 tablespoon organic sunflower oil
1 teaspoon sesame oil
250g/8oz oyster mushrooms or any others, roughly sliced
200g/7oz pak choi, trimmed and roughly sliced
Sea salt and freshly ground black pepper
1 tablespoon finely chopped coriander leaves

*Coeliacs please use gluten-free ingredients

Whisk the first four ingredients together in a small bowl. Heat the oils in a large deep frying pan or wok. Add the mushrooms, fry for a couple of minutes, then add the pak choi and cook over medium heat until the mushrooms are golden brown.

Stir in the soy mixture and bring to the boil for a couple of seconds so that the sauce cooks. Season to taste with salt and pepper. Serve immediately with a sprinkling of coriander.

Broccoli and Cauliflower Gratin Serves 4

You can use organic frozen vegetables for this gratin but fresh is best. This recipe avoids the usual butter and flour white sauce altogether and instead uses fat-free fromage frais and grated cheese to the same effect.

1 medium head of broccoli
1 medium head of cauliflower
250ml/1 cup half-fat crème fraîche
Sea salt and freshly ground black pepper
A little freshly grated nutmeg
115g/4oz reduced-fat hard cheese, grated
1 teaspoon Dijon mustard*
1 teaspoon Worcestershire sauce*
A sprinkling of cayenne pepper

* Coeliacs please use gluten-free ingredients

Preheat the oven to 200C/400F/Gas mark 6

Break the broccoli and cauliflower into florets and cook them in a pan of boiling water until just cooked but still slightly crunchy. Drain the vegetables, pat dry with absorbent kitchen paper and arrange them evenly in a heatproof serving dish.

In a bowl, mix the crème fraîche with the salt, pepper, nutmeg, half the grated cheese, the mustard and Worcestershire sauce. Spoon dollops of the mixture all over the broccoli and cauliflower then sprinkle with the remaining cheese and the cayenne.

Bake in the oven for about 15 minutes until golden and bubbling. Serve the gratin hot as an accompaniment to other dishes or just with baked or new potatoes.

Celeriac Purée Serves 4

This is such a light purée that you can use it to top pies and dishes that would normally use mashed potato. Any leftovers can be whizzed up with vegetable stock and freshly ground black pepper into a delicious soup. I serve this purée with most of the meat and game dishes in this book.

Juice of ½ a lemon
1 large celeriac, peeled and cut into cubes
30g/1oz reduced-fat butter or margarine-style spread
A pinch of sea salt and freshly ground black pepper
A sprinkling of freshly grated nutmeg

Bring a pan of water to the boil and add the lemon juice and celeriac. Cook until the celeriac is soft. Drain the celeriac and cool slightly before whizzing to a purée in a food processor. Add the butter, salt, pepper and nutmeg and whiz briefly again. Serve the purée in a warm dish.

Potato and Fennel Dauphinoise Serves 4

A potato Dauphinoise would normally have lashings of butter and thick cream. In this recipe I have tried to reduce the fat but maintain the flavour and texture.

You can serve the Dauphinoise with any other vegetarian dishes or just with a bowl of steamed or roast mixed seasonal vegetables.

500g/1lb 2oz potatoes, preferably Desiree
2 bulbs fennel, any tough layers removed
250ml/1 cup Elmlea light double cream (or the same amount of half-fat crème fraîche works well)
125ml/½ cup skimmed milk
2 garlic cloves, peeled and crushed
Sea salt and freshly ground black pepper
A little freshly grated nutmeg
30cm/12in wide x 5cm/2in deep ovenproof serving dish

Preheat the oven to 180C/350F/Gas mark 4.

Peel and very thinly slice the potatoes (I usually do this with the attachment in the food processor but you can do it by hand if you have time and a sharp knife). Slice the fennel very thinly.

Combine the cream, milk, garlic, salt, plenty of pepper, and nutmeg in a bowl.

Arrange the potatoes and fennel in alternate layers in the dish until there is only the final layer of potatoes left to add. Pour three quarters of the cream mixture over the potatoes and fennel. Top with the final layer of potatoes, making sure that the top looks neat. Now pour over the remaining cream mixture.

Bake in the oven for about 1¼ hours until the vegetables are soft and the top is golden and bubbling.

desserts

Carpaccio of Fresh Pineapple with Mint Sauce

Serves 8

The further into the south of France we drove on our honeymoon, the hotter the weather became and so we could enjoy candle-lit dinners on the terrace overlooking the gardens and mountains. We did find that higher temperatures put us off very rich puddings, so here is a light, fat-free one, which we very much enjoyed in a superb château in Provence.

1 large, ripe pineapple, trimmed and peeled
A handful of fresh coriander leaves
Finely grated rind and juice of 2 unwaxed limes
1 heaped tablespoon finely grated root ginger (remember to peel it first)
4 handfuls fresh mint leaves
2 tablespoons white rum
250ml/1 cup unsweetened pineapple juice
Fresh sprigs of little mint leaves, to decorate

Slice the pineapple into wafer thin slices using an extremely sharp, long knife. Please do this slowly and carefully. Then, using a small knife, remove the inner core from each slice and discard it. Arrange the pineapple in rows over a white plate or a glass dish.

Put the coriander leaves, lime rind and juice, grated root ginger, mint leaves, rum and pineapple juice into a food processor. Mix very briefly, so that it has the consistency of a ready-made mint sauce. Spoon the sauce over the pineapple and serve immediately for ultimate freshness. Decorate with the extra mint leaves.

Fruit Salad in Maple Syrup with Ginger Shortbread

Serves 4

I always think that putting fruit salad in a cookbook is a bit of a cheat but the delicate flavour of the maple syrup and the hint of ginger in both the salad and shortbread makes this one worth including. Anyone with willpower (not me!) can give their guests the shortbread and just stick to the fruit salad.

Ginger Shortbread

100g/¾ cup wheat-free flour*
1 teaspoon finely grated root ginger
55g/scant ⅔ cup ground almonds
100g/3½ oz butter
55g/⅓ cup unrefined caster sugar

Fruit salad

2 ripe peaches or nectarines, peeled and stoned and sliced (or 2 peeled and sliced kiwi fruit and 2 stoned, sliced plums)
1 sweet apple, peeled, quartered, cored and finely sliced
1 sweet ripe pear, peeled, quartered, cored and finely sliced
155g/5½ oz chopped fresh pineapple flesh
1 small ripe mango, peeled and cut into cubes
Juice of 1 orange
½ teaspoon very finely grated root ginger
1 tablespoon maple syrup

*Coeliacs please use gluten-free ingredients

Preheat the oven to 160C/325F/Gas mark 3.

Put all the ingredients for the shortbread in a food processor and pulse until you progress from fine breadcrumbs to a soft dough. This takes a few minutes.

Remove the dough with a spatula. Pat it out on a non-stick baking sheet into a round and then smooth out with a rolling pin into a neat circle.

Using a sharp knife, score lines to mark 8 wedges and prick lightly with a fork. Alternatively, you can roll out a thinner rectangle and cut 12 squares.

Bake in the oven for about 15–20 minutes until golden but not brown. Cool slightly before cutting the shortbread along the score lines. Leave the shortbread until cold and then break up into the segments and serve.

The shortbread will keep in an airtight container for at least a week, but remember – just one piece!

Mix all the prepared fruit together in a serving bowl and stir in the orange juice, ginger and maple syrup. Serve within a few hours of making so that the fruit looks fresh and appealing. Keep the fruit salad chilled and covered in the refrigerator until needed.

Spiced Fruit in Mulled Wine Serves 12

This is a lovely warming winter pudding – just what is needed in the bleak mid-winter. You can imagine roaring log fires, Christmas decorations and carol singers. Make it the day before serving for the best results.

Spiced fruit salad

500ml/2 cups light red wine
250ml/1 cup water
250ml/1 cup port
125ml/½ cup runny orange blossom honey
800g/1lb 12oz mixed dried fruits (apricots, peaches, pears, apples, prunes and figs)
100g/¾ cup raisins or sultanas
1 vanilla pod, split
2 cinnamon sticks
2 bay leaves
8 cloves
2.5cm/1in piece root ginger, peeled and sliced
Finely grated rind of ½ an unwaxed orange

To serve (optional)

Virtually fat-free fromage frais mixed with the finely grated rind of up to 1 unwaxed orange

Combine all the ingredients for the spiced fruit salad in a big bowl, cover and leave in a cool place overnight.

Transfer the fruit salad to a large pan and cook over medium heat until it reaches boiling point, then lower the heat and simmer for about 30 minutes until the fruits are soft and plump.

Strain the fruit salad over a serving bowl and remove the vanilla pod, cinnamon, bay leaves, cloves and ginger. Add the fruit back to the mulled wine in the serving bowl.

Serve with a bowl of fromage frais flavoured with some grated orange.

Little Apple Pots Serves 4

A sugar-free pudding is not only great for the figure but better for children too, so this makes a great little pudding for all the family.

6 ripe eating apples, stalks removed
1½ tablespoons porridge oat flakes*
½ teaspoon ground cinnamon
250g/1 cup virtually fat-free fromage frais

*Coeliacs please use gluten-free ingredients

Preheat the oven to 200C/400F/Gas mark 6

Score a thin line around the middle of each apple; this prevents them bursting in the oven. Place the apples in an ovenproof dish and bake until they are puffy and soft – about 35 minutes depending on the size and variety.

When the apples have cooled enough to be able to touch them, peel off the skins and discard. Scrape the flesh off the cores and transfer it to a bowl. Mash the apple with a fork and set aside to cool.

Preheat the grill, scatter the porridge oat flakes over a baking tray, sprinkle with cinnamon and toast until it starts to colour and smell nutty.

Spoon the cold mashed apple into four glasses (short tumblers for children and martini or wine glasses for adults). Gently spread the fromage frais over the top and then sprinkle with the cooled porridge oat flakes. Cover and chill until needed.

Apple and Ginger Upside Down Pudding Serves 6

This pudding uses low-fat butter or margarine so that the recipe is lower in fat than the standard version. Like most puddings, however, it does contain sugar and calories so a small helping is recommended.

3 large ripe eating apples, peeled, cut into eight and cored
4 heaped tablespoons ginger preserve
115g/4oz reduced-fat butter or margarine-style spread
115g/½ generous cup unrefined caster sugar
1 large free-range egg
155g/1¼ cups wheat-free flour*
3 teaspoons wheat-free baking powder*
2 teaspoons finely grated root ginger
3 tablespoons apple juice
Virtually fat-free fromage frais (optional)

*Coeliacs please use gluten-free ingredients

Preheat the oven to 180C/350F/Gas mark 4.

Arrange the apples all over the base of a deep-sided 25cm/10 inch ovenproof serving dish. Dot the ginger preserve over the apple pieces.

In a food processor, blend together the butter or margarine and sugar for a few seconds then briefly whiz in the egg and then the flour, baking powder and ginger. Pulse in the apple juice and then scrape the mixture out of the bowl with a spatula and spread evenly over the apples.

Bake in the oven for about 45 minutes until the sponge looks golden and feels springy to the touch. Serve the pudding hot or warm.

Cranberry and Wine Jelly with Grapes Serves 4-6

Mix red and white grapes for a pretty effect in this dish. Alternatively, choose any fruit in season and serve, fresh or poached, around the jellies.

300ml/1¼ cups red wine
140g/¾ cup unrefined caster sugar
Finely grated rind of 1 unwaxed orange
1 teaspoon mixed spice*
A sprig of rosemary
600ml/2½ cups cranberry juice
1½ sachets/US 1½ tablespoons powdered gelatine or vegetarian equivalent
A fresh bunch of red seedless grapes, skinned and halved
2–3 tablespoons redcurrant jelly
Juice of 1 large orange
A little red wine or port
4–6 ramekin dishes or tin jelly moulds, lightly brushed with oil

*Coeliacs please use gluten-free ingredients

Stir the wine, sugar, orange rind, mixed spice and rosemary together in a saucepan over medium heat to gently dissolve the sugar. Bring the mixture to the boil and boil for 5 minutes. Remove the pan from the heat, add the cranberry juice and allow the mixture to infuse for 5 minutes.

Place the saucepan back onto medium heat and bring the cranberry and wine mixture to the boil. Boil for 5 minutes, then remove from the heat and quickly stir in the gelatine. Stir from time to time until the gelatine has dissolved.

Sieve the jelly into a good pouring jug and then pour the wine jelly into the prepared ramekins. Leave the jellies to set for at least 4 hours or until firm enough to turn out.

Meanwhile, prepare as many of the grapes as you think you will need for your guests and put them in a bowl.

Place the redcurrant jelly, orange juice and a little extra wine or port in a saucepan and bring it to the boil to dissolve the jelly. Adjust the consistency with more liquid or jelly if necessary – it should be just runny enough to coat the grapes. Quickly remove it from the heat and blend thoroughly until smooth.

Pour it over the grapes, cool and then cover it and leave at room temperature until ready to serve. Turn out the jellies onto plates and spoon the grapes, with a little of the liquid, around each jelly. Serve straight away.

Pears in Marsala and Cinnamon Serves 4

Italians always seem to have recipes for peaches in various liqueurs or Marsala, so it is rather nice to find a delicious pear recipe on the same theme.

4 ripe well-rounded pears

30g/1oz reduced-fat butter or margarine-style spread, at room temperature

1 tablespoon orange blossom honey

½ teaspoon ground cinnamon

200ml/¾ cup Marsala

Virtually fat-free fromage frais or half-fat crème fraîche (optional)

Preheat the oven to 180C/350F/Gas mark 4.

Cut a small slice from the rounded end of each pear so that it will stand up. Spread a little butter over the skin of each pear and stand them in an ovenproof dish. Sprinkle with the honey and cinnamon and pour over the Marsala. Cover loosely with foil and bake for about 1 hour until tender.

Serve the pears warm with all the lovely juices. Fromage frais or crème fraîche is a delicious accompaniment if your guests are not on a rigid diet.

Melon Sorbet Serves 6

Root ginger adds a lovely flavour to this sorbet. It may look rather unappealing, but root ginger has a delicious scent that is lemony and spicy at the same time. As well as its culinary value, it has great medicinal value and I love drinking hot water and ginger every winter morning.

½ ripe galia melon, seeded and flesh cut into small pieces
Juice of 1 large lemon
1 tablespoon finely grated root ginger
4 tablespoons unrefined caster sugar
1 free-range egg white, stiffly beaten in a large bowl

An ice cream maker is needed for this recipe

Liquidize the melon with the lemon juice, ginger and sugar until smooth. You should have 700ml/3 cups of purée but if not just add a little water. Using a metal spoon, fold the purée into the beaten egg white, a little at a time, then transfer the mixture to a prepared ice cream maker and churn until softly frozen.

Scoop the sorbet out of the machine, seal it in a container and freeze until needed.

Blood Orange and Rosewater Sorbet Serves 6

This is a refreshing pudding to follow a hearty casserole or an oriental dish, and is particularly delicious served with Ginger Shortbread (see page 172). Blood oranges are available in January and February.

200g/¾ cup unrefined caster sugar
200ml/¾ cup rosewater (available in supermarkets or pharmacies)
600ml/2½ cups fresh blood orange juice
Finely grated rind of ½ a blood orange
A squeeze of lemon juice

An ice cream maker is needed for this recipe

Place the sugar and rosewater in a pan and simmer over low heat until the mixture is slightly syrupy. Leave it to cool. Put the orange juice into a large bowl and stir in the syrup.

Stir in the orange rind and a squeeze of lemon juice and leave to cool completely.

Transfer the mixture to your ice cream maker and churn the sorbet until softly frozen. Scrape the sorbet out of the machine into a container, seal and freeze until needed.

Lemon Amaretti Creams Serves 6

You will be amazed at how quick and easy this recipe is. It is this year's emergency standby pudding for unexpected guests who, after several glasses of wine, decide to stay on to dinner! I always keep Amaretti biscuits in the store cupboard, lemons and virtually fat-free fromage frais in the refrigerator, so it is only the lemon curd that I have to remember to buy.

325g/11½ oz jar luxury lemon curd*
750g/3 cups virtually fat-free fromage frais
Finely grated rind of ½ an unwaxed lemon (plus a little extra for decoration)
8 Amaretti morbidi (wheat-free soft almond macaroons)*, broken into quarters

*Coeliacs please use gluten-free ingredients

Mix together the first three ingredients in the given order in a mixing bowl using a metal spoon. Fold in the Amaretti pieces and spoon the cream into six small wine glasses. Decorate with a tiny splash of finely grated lemon rind, cover and chill until needed.

Peach and Blueberry Pie Serves 6

You can make this pie with any fruit combination that you like – apple and raisin or pear and blackberry are just two suggestions. Use whichever fruit is in season and then you will enjoy the best flavours at a good price.

Pastry

300g/2½ cups wheat-free flour*
170g/6oz butter
1 free-range egg
A little rosewater (available in supermarkets or pharmacies)

Filling

420g/15oz can sliced peaches in fruit juice, drained
255g/9oz blueberries
55g/ scant ⅔ cup ground almonds
75g/ scant ½ cup unrefined caster sugar
½ teaspoon ground cinnamon
A little extra unrefined caster sugar and ground cinnamon for dusting
22cm/8½ in non-stick, fluted, loose-bottomed flan tin for a warm or cold pie or a quiche dish for a hot pie

*Coeliacs please use gluten-free products

Preheat oven to 190C/375F/Gas mark 5.

Make the pastry by mixing the flour and butter in a food processor until it resembles breadcrumbs. Add the egg, whiz briefly and then add a little rosewater – just enough so that the dough comes together into a ball. Wrap the dough in clingfilm and chill.

Mix the peaches, blueberries, almonds, sugar and cinnamon together in a large bowl.

Divide the pastry into two portions of two-thirds and one-third.

On a floured surface, roll out the larger portion of pastry into a circle large enough to line the prepared tin. Line the tin with the pastry, trim the edges flat with a sharp knife, prick the base with a fork in half a dozen places and then fill with the fruit mixture.

Roll out the remaining pastry into a circle large enough to cover the pie. Trim and gently neaten the edges. Make a small hole in the centre of the pie for the steam to escape and sprinkle the pie with the extra sugar and cinnamon mixture.

Bake in the oven for about 35 minutes until the pastry is golden. Let the pie cool completely, then carefully lift it out of the tin, remove the base and slide it onto a serving dish. Warm the pie through if you like, just before serving. Alternatively, serve the pie hot in the quiche dish.

Creamed Rice Terrine with Summer Berry Sauce

Serves 8

This recipe is so easy – just a couple of cans of rice pudding and a packet of frozen summer berries. If you chill it in the deep freeze for 20 minutes and then transfer it to the refrigerator it will be ready to serve in another 20 minutes.

1 x 11.7g sachet/US 1 tablespoon powdered gelatine, dissolved in 3 tablespoons water according to the instructions
2 x 425g/15oz cans 99% fat-free rice pudding (Sainsbury's is gluten-free)
1 teaspoon pure vanilla extract
500g/1lb 2oz bag frozen summer berries, defrosted
22cm/8½ in long non-stick loaf tin, lined with clingfilm so that it hangs over all the sides.

Dissolve the gelatine in a small bowl according to the instructions on the packet. Empty the cans of rice pudding into another bowl and mix together briefly. Stir the dissolved gelatine and then the vanilla into the rice.

Secure the clingfilm so that it doesn't slip down the sides of the tin and pour in the rice pudding. Freeze the creamed rice terrine in the freezer for about 25 minutes before transferring to the refrigerator to set firmly.

Liquidize the berries and juices until you have a smooth sauce. Turn the rice pudding out of the loaf tin onto a long serving dish and peel off the clingfilm. Serve immediately with a little of the sauce drizzled over and serve the remaining sauce separately.

Grown-up Lychee and Lime Jelly Serves 6–8

Children and adults alike will love this tangy jelly with lots of healthy fruit, so it's ideal for a family lunch in the summer. It is refreshing, quick and easy to make. Vanilla ice cream is a perfect accompaniment for the children but should be avoided by the grown-ups!

Jelly

2 x 135g/4½ oz packets lime flavour jelly

425g/15oz can lychees in light syrup or fresh lychees if you can get them

4 fresh unwaxed limes

Fresh fruit salad (optional)

Lychees, strawberries, mango, pineapple or kiwi are delicious with the jelly

Small sprigs of fresh mint to decorate

1kg/2lb non-stick loaf tin, lightly oiled

Boil 625ml/2½ cups of water. Put the jelly into a bowl and pour over the boiling water. Stir until dissolved.

Drain the lychees and pat dry with absorbent kitchen paper.

Finely grate the rind of two of the limes into the jelly. Now squeeze the juice from all four limes and add to the jelly. Pour the jelly into the prepared tin, chill for 10 minutes in the freezer for speed, and then transfer it to the refrigerator.

When the jelly has thickened enough to hold the lychees, push them down into the jelly, using clean fingers, distributing them attractively. Leave to set. Keep the jelly chilled in the refrigerator until needed. Turn it out on to a rectangular plate and surround it with the fresh fruit salad and little sprigs of fresh mint.

Guilt-free Toffee Puddings Serves 4

This is as guilt-free a toffee pudding as I can manage and it certainly makes you feel that you have indulged yourself and had a special treat. Guests can have reduced-fat vanilla ice cream or half-fat creme fraiche as an accompaniment.

200g/7oz pitted dried dates
6 tablespoons freshly squeezed orange juice
1 teaspoon vanilla extract
1 teaspoon mixed spice*
2 free-range eggs, separated
85g/⅔ cup self-raising wheat-free flour* OR plain wheat-free flour* with 1 heaped teaspoon of wheat-free baking powder*
8 tablespoons 100% pure maple syrup
Virtually fat-free crème fraîche, to serve (optional)
You will need 4 large ramekins or tin moulds

*Coeliacs please use gluten-free ingredients

Preheat the oven to 180C/350F/Gas mark 4.

Put the dates in a pan with 185ml/1¼ cups of water and the orange juice. Bring to the boil and cook for about 10 minutes until the dates are softened and some of the liquid has evaporated. Cool the mixture, transfer it to a food processor, add the vanilla and mixed spice and blend briefly.

Very briefly whiz in the egg yolks followed by the self-raising flour or the plain flour and baking powder. Transfer this mixture to a bowl.

In another bowl whisk the egg whites until stiff and then fold them into the date mixture using a metal spoon.

Put 2 tablespoons of maple syrup in each prepared ramekin or tin mould and then spoon the mixture over and cover tightly with tin foil. Stand the ramekins/moulds in a shallow pan of hot water (to about half-way up the ramekin/mould) and bake in the oven for about 50 minutes.

Let them cool for about 5 minutes, then carefully peel off the foil and test they are cooked by inserting a skewer into the pudding – if it comes out clean they are cooked. Loosen the puddings by running a knife around the edge, invert them onto warm plates and serve them hot on their own or with a dollop of crème fraîche.

Lavender Summer Pudding Serves 6

The best results for this pudding came from using the gluten-free bread that is part of my Signature series (see page 175 for stockists). However, you can use wheat-free white bread as an alternative.

1kg/2¼ lb frozen (thawed) or fresh summer berries such as strawberries, raspberries, blackberries, black and red currants
425ml/1⅔ cups red vermouth
Juice and finely grated rind of 1 small unwaxed orange
1 tablespoon fresh lavender flowers, washed in cold water
2 heaped tablespoons unrefined caster sugar
1 tablespoon wheat-free cornflour* dissolved in 1 tablespoon cold water
2 tablespoons distilled lavender water
1 loaf gluten-free white bread (from the Signature series if possible)
Some little sprigs of fresh lavender for decoration
900ml/4-cup pudding basin

*Coeliacs please use gluten-free ingredients

If you are using frozen fruit, let the juices drain into a dish so that you can use them in the recipe. Put any juices with the vermouth, orange juice and rind, lavender flowers and sugar into a non-stick saucepan and bring to the boil. Turn down the heat and simmer until the liquid is reduced by half. Stir in the dissolved cornflour, bring to the boil and simmer for 1 minute. As soon as the sauce is very thick and clear, take the pan off the heat. Remove the sprigs of lavender and discard them.

Stir the lavender water and all the fruit into the thick sauce and leave it to cool. The fruit will inevitably let out more juices, so the sauce must be very thick. If you have any doubts then add a little more dissolved cornflour and boil up again before adding the lavender water and berries.

Slice the bread very thinly, trim the crusts off and discard. Cut the slices diagonally into halves. Line the bottom and sides of the pudding basin with the triangles of bread. When the berry mixture is cold, fill the lined basin with the mixture; cover the fruit with the remaining bread. Place a plate directly on top of the bread – it should just fit into the basin and cover the bread completely. Press the plate down with a weight or a heavy can. Put the basin onto a larger plate to catch any overflowing juices, and chill the pudding in the refrigerator for 8-24 hours.

Just before serving, turn the pudding onto a large plate and decorate with sprigs of fresh lavender. If you turn the pudding out too early, it might collapse or bulge slightly, so it is better left to the last minute to guarantee perfect results.

Rosewater Angel Cake with Berries Serves 6–12

This is a low-fat cake, so it is ideal for weight-watching dinner guests. You can use any mixture of fruit you like to suit whatever is in season. I have left the quantities for the filling and sauce optional so that you can use this recipe for a small party of six guests or increase the amount for the maximum of 12 guests.

Cake

125g/1 cup rice flour, sifted

185g/ scant 1 cup unrefined caster sugar

A pinch of fine salt

7 large free-range egg whites

2 teaspoons cream of tartar

1 tablespoon rosewater

Filling and sauce

Plenty of fresh soft fruits such as strawberries, blackberries, blueberries, raspberries, stoned cherries or currants

White rum

Unrefined caster sugar to taste

A large, deep, non-stick ring baking tin or a large, deep, non-stick Kugelhopf tin

Preheat the oven to 180C/350F/Gas mark 4.

Make the cake first. Sift together the flour, 7 tablespoons of the sugar and the salt in a bowl and set aside. In another larger bowl, whisk the egg whites at low speed for about 1 minute until they are thick and foamy. Add the cream of tartar and increase the speed to medium. Slowly sprinkle 2 more tablespoons of sugar into the egg whites and beat them until they form soft peaks. Add the rosewater and fold in the remaining sugar, followed by the sifted flour mixture.

Pour the cake mixture into the tin and bake in the oven for about 40 minutes, or until an inserted skewer comes out clean. It should be golden and firm to touch.

Leave the cake to cool in the tin for 20 minutes, after which time the cake should have come away from the sides of the tin. Ease the cake out and turn it onto a large serving plate. Fill the centre of the cake with as many berries as you like, so that it looks pretty. Keep the rest to make the sauce.

Put plenty of berries, some rum and a little sugar into the food processor and pulse to a purée. Adjust the sweetness and the consistency to suit your taste with extra sugar, water and rum. Sieve the sauce and discard all the pips and skins. The sauce should be just runny enough to spoon over the cake and trickle a little bit down the sides of the cake, but not too runny otherwise it will trickle away. Spoon the sauce decoratively over the sponge ring only, not on the fruit filling.

Serve the rest of the sauce in a pretty jug to accompany the pudding.

cakes, breads and cookies

Low-Fat Ginger Flapjacks Serves 6

You can use whichever dried fruits you have in the cupboard – the more exotic the better! Use organic oats as they give a nuttier taste as well as being better for you. If you prefer a subtle ginger flavour, reduce the amount of root and stem ginger according to taste.

255g/2½ cups organic quick-cooking oats*
55g/ scant ¼ cup unrefined soft brown sugar
5 tablespoons skimmed milk powder
A pinch of salt
55g/⅓ cup grated root ginger
55g/⅓ cup chopped stem ginger
55g/⅓ cup glacé mango pieces
1 tablespoon fresh lemon juice
2 tablespoons skimmed milk
6 generous tablespoons golden syrup from a warmed spoon
1 free-range egg white
23cm/9in non-stick baking tin, lined with baking parchment

*Coeliacs please use gluten-free ingredients

Preheat the oven to 190C/375F/Gas mark 5.

Place the oats, sugar, milk powder and salt in a bowl and mix them together. Stir in the grated ginger and stem ginger, followed by the mango, lemon juice and milk. Lastly, add the syrup and blend it all together. Whisk the egg white until foamy but not stiff, then fold it into the dry mixture.

Spoon the mixture into the prepared tin and press it down firmly, especially around the sides. Bake for about 25 minutes until dark golden brown and firm. Leave the flapjacks to cool slightly before cutting into slices or triangles.

Blackberry and Lemon Muffins

Muffins are perfect for breakfast at the weekend, when you can enjoy them while relaxing with the papers. Alternatively, you can serve them with a large fresh fruit salad for a quick and easy lunch.

285g/2¼ cups wheat-free flour*
1 tablespoon wheat-free baking powder*
115g/½ cup unrefined caster sugar
1 large free-range egg
250ml/1 cup low-fat, natural live yogurt
4 tablespoons organic sunflower oil (don't use cold pressed as it is too strong)
Finely grated rind of ½ an unwaxed lemon
170g/1½ cups fresh or lightly thawed frozen blackberries (without any juice)
12-cup muffin tin lined with 12 paper cases

*Coeliacs please use gluten-free ingredients.

Preheat the oven to 200C/400F/Gas mark 6.

Sift the flour and baking powder into a mixing bowl and stir in the sugar. Make a well in the centre of the mixture. Mix the egg, yogurt, oil and grated lemon in a separate bowl, then quickly pour and stir it into the flour mixture. Stir lightly until just combined. Do not over-mix or the muffins will be heavy.

Lightly fold in the blackberries with a metal spoon.

Spoon the mixture into the paper cases. Bake the muffins for about 20 minutes until they have risen and are golden brown and firm.

Transfer them to a wire rack and serve warm or cold. The muffins are best eaten fresh, on the day they were baked, but can be kept in an airtight container in the refrigerator for a few days.

Soda Bread Serves 8

Now that I know I can buy buttermilk in my local supermarket, I make this soda bread all the time. Like all soda breads, it really should be eaten on the day it is made – that way you do not need to have any butter with it.

350g/2¾ cups wheat-free flour*
125g/1 cup fine oatmeal*
2 heaped teaspoons bicarbonate of soda
1 heaped teaspoon wheat-free baking powder*
½ teaspoon fine salt
1 heaped teaspoon runny honey
300ml/1 cup and 2 tablespoons buttermilk
60ml/¼ cup skimmed milk (more or less as necessary to suit the flour absorbency)
Extra skimmed milk for brushing

*Coeliacs please use gluten-free ingredients

Preheat the oven to 200C/400F/Gas mark 6.

Combine all the dry ingredients in a big bowl and make a well in the centre. Mix the honey, buttermilk and skimmed milk together in a small bowl. Pour the mixture into the dry ingredients and use a metal spoon to mix it all into a lumpy mass. Now use your (clean) hands to knead the mixture into a dough.This will take a couple of minutes.

Transfer the dough to a clean, floured surface and knead for another couple of minutes.

Shape the dough into a 20cm/8 inch round and place it on a non-stick baking sheet. Use a sharp knife to cut a deep cross in the top of the dough and divide it into a total of eight deep portions. Brush with a little extra skimmed milk. Bake for about 35 minutes until golden and slightly risen. Cool the bread on a wire rack.

Lime Roulade

Serves 10

Everyone thinks you have made a huge effort if you present them with a roulade. They are, however, quick and easy to make once you have made one and got the hang of it. You can serve the roulade with a bowl of fresh raspberries or strawberries in summer.

Roulade

4 large free-range egg whites
115g/½ cup unrefined caster sugar, plus extra for dusting
75g/generous ½ cup wheat-free flour*
Finely grated rind of 1 unwaxed lime
3 teaspoons fresh lime juice

Filling

2 heaped tablespoons reduced-sugar strawberry or raspberry jam
4 heaped tablespoons virtually fat-free fromage frais
Finely grated rind of ½ an unwaxed lime
A little extra unrefined caster sugar for dusting and a few fresh strawberries or raspberries for decoration (optional)
28 x 35cm/11 x 14in Swiss roll tin lined with baking parchment

*Coeliacs please use gluten-free ingredients

Preheat the oven to 150C/300F/Gas mark 2.

Beat the egg whites in a large bowl with an electric mixer until stiff, then gradually beat in the sugar. Fold in the flour, then the lime rind and juice. Spread the mixture lightly in the prepared tin, taking it into all the corners. Bake in the centre of the oven for 7–10 minutes until golden and springy to the touch.

Lay a sheet of baking parchment on a clean surface and dust it lightly with the extra caster sugar. Remove the cooked roulade from the oven and quickly loosen the edges of the cake so that it comes away from the paper. Immediately invert the roulade onto the sugared paper and pull off the lining paper. Cover the roulade with a clean cloth and leave it to go cold.

When you are ready to fill the roulade, remove the cloth and spread a thin layer of jam evenly all over the inside of the cake.

Place the fromage frais in a bowl, beat for a few seconds with a spoon and then incorporate the grated lime. Spread the fromage frais over the jam and roll up the roulade. Slide it on to a serving dish using the paper to guide you, then remove the paper and discard.

Sprinkle the roulade with a little extra unrefined caster sugar and serve decorated with a few large sliced strawberries or some whole raspberries.

Blackberry and Apple Cake Serves 10

I love to go blackberry picking along the fields and lanes of Norfolk with my little dog. It is the only time of year that he gets bored on our walks as I can't bear to miss one blackberry that is within my reach but as far as my dog is concerned hedgerows lose their appeal after an hour or two!

200g/2 cups peeled, cored and chopped eating apples
170g/1 cup finely grated carrot
255g/2¼ cups fresh or frozen blackberries
250ml/1 cup cranberry juice
140g/generous 1 cup buckwheat flour
140g/generous 1 cup maize flour
3 teaspoons wheat-free baking powder*
A pinch of fine salt
1 teaspoon ground cinnamon
2 teaspoons mixed spice*
2 large free-range egg whites, lightly beaten
170g/1 cup unrefined soft brown sugar, sifted
1kg/2lb non-stick loaf tin, lined with baking parchment

*Coeliacs please use gluten-free ingredients

Preheat the oven to 180C/350F/Gas mark 4.

Place the apple, carrot, blackberries and cranberry juice in a non-stick saucepan, bring to the boil and then set aside to cool.

Sift the flours, baking powder, salt and spices into a bowl. In a separate bowl, whisk the egg whites until stiff, then gradually whisk in the sugar until you have a stiff meringue.

Stir the fruit mixture into the flour mixture and then fold in the meringue. Spoon the mixture into the prepared baking tin and gently smooth over the top.

Bake in the oven for about 1½ hours until the loaf is well-risen and golden brown. An inserted skewer should come out clean when the cake is cooked through.

Leave the cake to cool, then turn it out onto a wire rack and remove the paper. When the cake is completely cold, wrap in foil and store in an airtight container until needed.

Cranberry and Orange Angel Cake Serves 12

You can serve this cake on its own for tea or as a pudding. If you choose the pudding option, serve it with a big bowl of berries in a splash of the orange liqueur and a bowl of virtually fat-free fromage frais or seasonal fruit sauce.

115g/generous ¾ cup rice flour
285g/1½ cups unrefined caster sugar
10 free-range egg whites at room temperature
Generous ½ teaspoon cream of tartar
1 tablespoon orange liqueur
100g/½ cup cut, dried mixed peel
70g/½ cup dried and sweetened cranberries
½ teaspoon ground cinnamon
1 teaspoon unrefined caster sugar
A heart-shaped or standard non-stick angel cake tin, lined with baking parchment

Preheat the oven to 180C/350F/Gas mark 4.

Sift together the flour and 100g/¾ cup of the unrefined caster sugar into a bowl. In another bowl, beat the egg whites until foamy, add the cream of tartar and beat until they form soft peaks.

Beat 2 tablespoons at a time of the remaining sugar into the egg whites, until you have used up all the sugar and the meringue is glossy and stiff. Now fold in the liqueur and the mixed peel. Carefully sprinkle a little of the flour mixture over the meringue and gently fold it in. Continue this process until all the flour has been incorporated.

Spoon the meringue mixture into the prepared tin and sprinkle the cranberries over the top. Bake the cake for about 35 minutes until golden (an inserted skewer should come out clean if the cake is cooked through).

Allow the cake to cool a little in the tin, before turning out onto a wire rack. Mix the cinnamon with the teaspoon of unrefined caster sugar and sprinkle over the cake. Set aside to cool completely. The cake is best eaten fresh on the day.

Banana and Chocolate Loaf

Serves 10

This loaf is ideal for picnics, as it slices up very easily and keeps well in foil. The inclusion of chocolate means the recipe contains some fat but this is minimal – a mere 1 gram per slice. The loaf tastes even better the day after it is made.

2 medium-sized, very ripe bananas, peeled
200ml/¾ cup pure apple juice
60ml/¼ cup lemon juice
140g/generous 1 cup buckwheat flour
140g/generous 1 cup maize flour
3 teaspoons wheat-free baking powder*
A pinch of fine salt
2 large free-range egg whites
140g/ scant 1 cup soft brown sugar
30g/⅓ cup coarsely grated dark chocolate*
2 teaspoons pure chocolate extract (fat-free)
1kg/2.2lb non-stick loaf tin, lined with baking parchment

*Coeliacs please use gluten-free ingredients

Preheat the oven to 180C/350F/Gas mark 4.

In a small bowl, mash the bananas, apple juice and lemon juice together until completely blended. Sift together the flours, baking powder and salt in a separate bowl. In another bowl, beat the egg whites until stiff, then gradually whisk in the sugar.

Add the grated chocolate and chocolate extract to the banana mixture and stir the mixture into the dry ingredients. Now quickly fold in the meringue. Spoon the loaf mixture into the prepared tin and gently smooth over the top. Bake the loaf for 1 hour or until it is firm. (An inserted skewer should come out clean when the loaf is cooked through.)

Cool the loaf in the tin, then turn it out onto a wire rack and remove the paper. When the loaf is cold, wrap in foil and store in an airtight container until needed.

Fruit Cake Serves 12

Of all the cakes, fruit cake is the most nutritious as dried fruit provides a concentrated source of essential minerals, including iron. The sweetness of dried fruit comes from the natural sugar, or fructose, it contains – fruit cakes therefore require less sugar than other cakes.

130g/ scant 1 cup ready-to-eat dried figs, chopped
200g/1 cup ready-to-eat dried peaches, chopped
Finely grated rind of 1 unwaxed orange
250ml/1 cup unsweetened orange juice
2 heaped tablespoons organic golden syrup
225g/1¾ cups wheat-free flour*
2 teaspoons mixed spice *
2 teaspoons cinnamon
2 teaspoons wheat-free baking powder*
350g/2½ cups mixed dried fruit
75g/generous ½ cup dried cherries or cranberries
3 tablespoons brandy
3 large free-range egg whites
1 tablespoon reduced-sugar smooth apricot jam
20cm/8in round, loose-bottomed non-stick cake tin or a non-stick loaf tin, lightly greased and lined with baking parchment

*Coeliacs please use gluten-free ingredients

Preheat the oven to 180C/350F/Gas mark 4.

Combine the figs, peaches and orange rind in a saucepan. Pour in the orange juice and bring to the boil. Reduce the heat and simmer at bubbling point for about 10 minutes or until the fruit is very soft.

Cool the mixture and then transfer it to a food processor. Whiz the mixture until it becomes a purée, stir in the syrup and leave it to cool.

Meanwhile, sift the flour, spices and baking powder into a big bowl. Stir in the mixed dried fruits, dried cherries and brandy and make a well in the centre.

In a clean bowl, beat the egg whites until stiff. Spoon the fig mixture into the well in the flour-and-fruit mixture and mix well, gradually incorporating the flour. Using a metal spoon gently fold in the egg whites.

Transfer the cake mixture to the prepared tin, gently level the surface and cover the top of the tin loosely with foil or baking parchment. Bake for 45 minutes, then remove the foil or parchment and bake for 30 minutes more until a skewer, inserted in the cake, comes out clean.

Remove the cake from the oven, brush the top with apricot jam and let it cool in the tin. When the cake is cold, take it out of the tin and peel off the lining paper. Wrap the cake in foil and store it in an airtight container for at least 24 hours before eating.

Mango and Carrot Cake Serves 10

This recipe does not contain oil – unlike all the other carrot cake recipes that I have tried and tested – so it is has much less fat in it. The topping is ideal for afternoon tea with the family or friends but if you are making it for your kids or your own lunch box then omit the topping.

Cake

245g/2 cups wheat-free flour*
3 heaped teaspoons wheat-free baking powder*
175g/1 generous cup unrefined muscovado sugar
1 teaspoon ground cinnamon
1 teaspoon finely grated root ginger
1 teaspoon mixed spice*
115g/1 scant cup sultanas
115g/¾ cup diced fresh mango
455g/1lb carrots, peeled and grated
1 large free-range egg, beaten
250ml/1 cup skimmed milk

Topping

250g/1 cup virtually fat-free peach and passion fruit fromage frais (Onken)
Finely grated rind of ½ an unwaxed orange
A sprinkling of poppy seeds
22cm/8½ in loose-bottomed round cake tin, lined with baking parchment

*Coeliacs please use gluten-free ingredients

Preheat the oven to 180C/350F/ Gas mark 4.

Mix the flour, baking powder, sugar, cinnamon, root ginger, mixed spice, sultanas and mango in a big bowl and then stir in the grated carrot. In a separate bowl combine the egg with the milk and then stir it into the carrot mixture.

Transfer the cake mixture to the prepared tin, bake for about 55 minutes until the cake is golden and firm to touch. If you are not sure it is ready, insert a skewer into the centre of the cake – if it comes out clean the cake is cooked through.

Leave the cake to cool in the tin and then transfer it to a serving plate to cool completely. Mix the fromage frais and grated orange together in a small bowl, spread it over the top of the cold cake and sprinkle with the poppy seeds.

Ginger Shortbread Serves 8

When you are choosing ginger, look for shiny skin and a plump root. Avoid any that are wrinkled or have dried up tufts of fibre at the knobbly breaks.

You can serve this shortbread with the Blood Orange and Rosewater Sorbet recipe on page 142 and the Melon Sorbet on page 141. As the shortbread keeps for such a long time it is ideal for Christmas and advance planning – just double the quantities.

100g/¾ cup wheat-free flour*
1 teaspoon finely grated root ginger
55g/scant ⅔ cup ground almonds
100g/3½ oz butter
55g/⅓ cup unrefined caster sugar

*Coeliacs please use gluten-free ingredients

Preheat the oven to 160C/325F/Gas mark 3.

Make the shortbread by putting all the ingredients in a food processor and pulsing until it progresses from fine breadcrumbs to a soft dough. This takes a few minutes.

Remove the dough with a spatula, and then pat it out on a non-stick baking sheet into a round. Smooth it out with a rolling pin into a 22cm/8½ inch circle. Using a sharp knife score deep lines to mark 8 wedges, then prick lightly with a fork. Alternatively, you can roll out a thinner rectangle and mark out 12 squares.

Bake in the oven for about 20 minutes until golden but not brown. Cool slightly before cutting the shortbread along the score lines. Leave the shortbread until cold and then break up into the segments and serve.

The shortbread will keep in an airtight container for at least a week, but don't be tempted to have more than just one piece if you are watching your figure.

USEFUL ADDRESSES

Antoinette Savill has a new range of gourmet gluten-, wheat- and dairy-free foods made by Wellfoods Ltd called the Antoinette Savill Signature Series. At the time of writing the range is sold in Waitrose and Budgens supermarkets across England, some bakeries, a selection of health food shops and also by mail order directly from Wellfoods Ltd. All orders are delivered within 24 hours by courier.

Antoinette Savill has a website with news, helpful hints and recipes for 'wheat watchers'. The site also includes reviews of her other books, plus a credit card hotline for purchasing books from Harper Collins publishers and gluten-free foods from Wellfoods Ltd. Website: www.wheatwatchers.com

Antoinette Savill is now working alongside purerfoods.com whose site includes some of her recipes and video demonstrations of cooking with gluten-, wheat- and dairy-free ingredients to make delicious and simple dishes for all the family.

Website: www.purerfoods.com

Organizations:

Institute for Optimum Nutrition
Blades Court
Deodar Road
London SW15 2NU
Telephone: 020 8877 9993
(A very good quarterly magazine and a list of qualified nutritionists around the UK)

Coeliac Society
PO BOX 220
High Wycombe
Buckinghamshire HP11 2HY
Telephone: 01494 437278
(A very good quarterly magazine and a complete list of gluten-free products is available)

Berrydale Publishers
Berrydale House
5 Lawn Road
London NW3 2XS
Telephone: 020 7722 2866
(The Inside Story food and health magazine and press releases)

Purerfoods.com
36 Albemarle Street
London W1S 4JE
Fax: 0207499 7676
Email: team@purerfoods.com

Purerfoods.com is a directory of high quality foods retailed in Britain. Tested and recommended by a team of food scientists, nutritionists and dieticians, so that you can make an informed decision on what you eat. Much of the information is free. The full service for subscribers costs less than 20p per week.

Stockists:

Wellfoods Ltd
Unit 6 Mapplewell Business Park
Mapplewell
Barnsley
S75 6BP
Telephone: 01226 381712
Fax: 01226 381858
Website: www.bake-it.com
Email: Wellfoods@bake-it.com
(Nationwide delivery of gluten-free and wheat-free flour and the Antoinette Savill Signature series of gluten-, wheat- and dairy-free food range available by mail order)

Organics Direct Ltd
7 Willow Street
London EC2A 4BH
Telephone: 020 7729 2828
Website: www.organicsdirect.com

The Organic Food Shop
45 Broughton Street
Edinburgh EH1 3JU
Telephone: 0131 556 1772
(Nationwide delivery of 4,500 lines, including teas and cheeses)

Rococo
321 Kings Road
London SW3 5EP
Telephone: 020 7352 5857
(Suppliers of sugar-free and dairy-free chocolate)

Farmers' Markets
Telephone: 01225 787914
Website: www.farmersmarkets.net
The best places to buy fresh foods, straight from the producers – support them whenever you can. Find out where your local market is by visiting their website or telephoning.

Simply Organic Food Company Ltd
Freepost, Units Ab2-A6
New Covent Garden Market
London SW8 5YY
Telephone: 0845 1000 444
Fax: 020 7622 4447
Website: www.simplyorganic.net
Email: orders@simplyorganic.net
(Everything organic and also wheat or lactose-free products)
Delivery nationwide, open 24hrs and 7 days per week

INDEX OF RECIPES

SOUPS

STARTERS

FISH AND SEAFOOD

MEAT, POULTRY AND GAME

VEGETARIAN MAIN COURSES

VEGETABLES

DESSERTS

CAKES, BREADS AND COOKIES

Lose Wheat, Lose Weight

The Healthy Way to Feel Well and Look Fantastic!

Antoinette Savill and Dawn Hamilton Ph.D.

The New Allergy-Free Diet Plan with 60 Easy Recipes.

Eating wheat makes us 'bloat up' – and is often the cause of headaches, skin conditions, tiredness, digestive discomfort and needless weight gain. Lose wheat and you will lose weight. Cutting out wheat should be an easy route to weight-loss but the modern diet means wheat's often in every meal. This book offers:

- Nutritional information and a full explanation of why wheat-free works.
- Wheat's connection to all sorts of different symptoms, sugar sensitivity and cravings.
- Case histories from people whose lives have improved after switching to wheat-free.
- A diet that won't leave you feeling tired out and energy depleted.

'I just had to write to tell you how your book has transformed my life and that of my two work colleagues. I had all the symptoms of wheat intolerance, and had been feeling awful for years. Your book has been like a magic wand, that has changed me. We all feel wonderful, have more energy and all our symptoms have disappeared. The added bonus is that after years of struggling to lose weight I'm also doing that too. FANTASTIC!!! So thanks again on behalf of three very happy people.' Carole Kennett (aged 53 and feeling 43)

Antoinette Savill is a Glenfiddich award-winning cookery writer who suffers from multiple food allergies and is the author of the *Gluten, Wheat and Dairy Free Cookbook* and co-author of *Super Energy Detox*. She is committed to creating delicious recipes for allergy sufferers. She has launched a successful website and range of gluten-free foods. Antoinette is well-known to the Coeliac Society (42,000 members).

Dawn Hamilton Ph.D. was trained as a nutritional therapist by Patrick Holford. She also has a PhD in psychology from Cranfield University – where she specialised in effective ways of eliminating stress and promoting health. Dawn works with a wide range of personal development and complementary therapies and is the co-author of *Super Energy Detox*.

Super Energy Detox

21-day plan with 60 allergy-free recipes

Antoinette Savill and Dawn Hamilton Ph.D.

By the authors of *Lose Wheat, Lose Weight,* this detox plan tackles the issue of food intolerance and has special 21-day regimes for summer and winter.

In *Super Energy Detox,* award-winning cookery writer Antoinette Savill and nutritionist Dawn Hamilton show you the benefits of cleansing your system with their special 3-week Summer and Winter detox programmes. With general advice on how to detox as well as specific pointers for food intolerance sufferers, you can learn how to regain lost energy, improve your mood, and solve weight issues. It contains over 60 low-fat wheat-, dairy-, gluten- and yeast-free recipes, Tai Chi energy exercises and excellent advice to help you put the detox into practice.

'Most diet books are written by nutritionists who know very little about cooking. The great thing about Antoinette Savill is that she is a cookery writer who got into writing about food intolerance after discovering that she herself was a sufferer. You can confidently recommend any of her books.' The Bookseller

Antoinette Savill is a Glenfiddich award-winning cookery writer who suffers from multiple food allergies and is the author of the *Gluten, Wheat and Dairy Free Cookbook* and co-author of *Lose Wheat, Lose Weight.* She is committed to creating delicious recipes for allergy sufferers. She has launched a successful website and range of gluten-free foods. Antoinette is well-known to the Coeliac Society (42,000 members).

Dawn Hamilton Ph.D. was trained as a nutritional therapist by Patrick Holford. She also has a PhD in psychology from Cranfield University – where she specialised in effective ways of eliminating stress and promoting health. Dawn works with a wide range of personal development and complementary therapies and is the co-author of *Lose Wheat, Lose Weight.*

ISBN 0-00-713399-5

Gluten, Wheat and Dairy Free Cookbook

Over 200 allergy-free recipes, from the 'Sensitive Gourmet'
Antoinette Savill

New edition bringing together the full range of recipes from Antoinette Savill's *Sensitive Gourmet* books. Also includes a new selection of 25 ultra low-fat options.

Antoinette Savill's previous titles broke new ground in creative, cosmopolitan cookery for people suffering from sensitivity to wheat, dairy or gluten. Now both *The Sensitive Gourmet* and *More from the Sensitive Gourmet* are available as one book. All those with lactose and wheat sensitivity, coeliac disease, asthma and eczema or chronic fatigue will find the book invaluable. This new edition contains over 200 recipes, from light savoury snacks and soups, to meat, fish and vegetable dishes for dinner parties through to naughty puddings, cakes, and fresh home-made breads.